BROADCASTING
GENOCIDE

**Censorship, Propaganda & State-Sponsored
Violence in Rwanda 1990 – 1994**

BROADCASTING GENOCIDE

Censorship, Propaganda & State-Sponsored
Violence in Rwanda 1990 – 1994

ARTICLE 19
October 1996

CONTENTS

i

ACKNOWLEDGEMENTS

This report was written by LINDA KIRSCHKE, Africa Programme Researcher at ARTICLE 19.

Journalist FAUSTIN KAGAME, an ARTICLE 19 Consultant, contributed unpublished transcripts of RTLM from April 1994, which he recorded while in hiding during the first few weeks of the genocide. He has given ARTICLE 19 exclusive use of this material, which he painstakingly translated into French, a daunting task which required great courage. The transcripts were translated from French to English by Linda Kirschke and Saïd Essoulami.

The Introduction and Conclusion were written by Richard Carver, ARTICLE 19's Africa Programme Consultant. The Chapter on International Law, the Media and Genocide was written by Sandra Coliver, ARTICLE 19's Legal Programme Director.

This report was edited by Carmel Bedford, copy-edited by Liz Schofield and designed by Sue York.

ARTICLE 19 gratefully acknowledges the generous support received from UNICEF (Rwanda) and Swedish International Development Agency (SIDA) for the research, editing and publication of this report.

AUTHOR'S ACKNOWLEDGEMENTS

Many thanks are due to François-Xavier Nsanzuwera; Joseph Matata; Charles Ntampaka; Alison Des Forges, Human Rights Watch Consultant; Scott Campbell, from the International Human Rights Law Group, and Filip Reyntjens for their kind advice on this project. ARTICLE 19 is indebted to all those who were willing to share their very painful memories of the genocide in order to provide witness testimony on the atrocities of this period.

Glossary

Akazu

"The little house". A term commonly used to refer to the inner circle of President Juvénal Habyarimana.

APROSOMA

Association pour la promotion sociale des masses (Association for the Social Promotion of the Masses). A political party with mainly Hutu support which became active in the mid-1950s.

Arusha Accords

Peace agreement between the RPF and the Rwandan government signed in August 1993. Although never implemented by the government of President Juvénal Habyarimana, these accords established a power-sharing agreement between the MRND, the RPF and the internal opposition parties and called for the fusion of the RPA and the FAR on a 40%-60% basis.

Bagogwe

A Tutsi sub-group, mainly herdsmen, which has lived outside traditional Tutsi political structures since the 17th century. Between 300 and 1,000 were massacred by government authorities in 1991 and many more were targeted during the 1994 genocide.

bourgemestre

Mayor or official, appointed by the President, to head a *commune*. (See below)

cellule

Cell. Administrative divisions within *secteurs* (see below). These are each led by an elected committee of five people. The committees choose a *responsable de cellule* (cell leader) to represent them.

CDR	*Coalition pour la défense de la république* (Coalition for the Defence of the Republic). An extremist political party which was established in 1992. In late 1993, the CDR formed an alliance with extremists within the MRND.
CND	*Conseil national pour le développement* (National Council for Development). The term used to describe parliament from 1978 until August 1993, when the parliament was renamed the *assemblée nationale de transition* (Transitional National Assembly) under the Arusha Accords of August 1993. Yet the building where parliament was located continued to be referred to as the "CND" even after this point. From December 1993 and throughout the genocide, this building was used as the RPF headquarters in Kigali.
commune	Municipality. The second largest administrative division in Rwanda; there are 143 *commune*s in every *préfecture* (see below).
FAR	*Forces armées rwandaises* (Rwandan Armed Forces).
"Hutu Power" movement	An extremist movement which emerged in mid-1993 and created splits within most of the internal opposition parties. These formed alliances with extremists in the CDR and MRND. During the 1994 genocide, all the cabinet members presented as opposition party representatives were in fact from the "Power" wing of their respective parties.

Ibyitso	"Accomplice", under the government of Habyarimana and during the 1994 genocide frequently used to refer to Tutsi who were accused, often falsely, of supporting the RPF.
ICTR	International Criminal Tribunal for Rwanda.
Impuzamugambi	Literally means, "Those with a single purpose". A militia affiliated with the CDR.
Interahamwe	"Those who work together." A militia affiliated with the MRND. It was established in 1992 and became more active in late 1993. Highly structured and centrally organized, this group played an important role in the 1994 genocide.
Inyenzi	"Cockroaches", an abusive term originally used for guerrillas who launched attacks on Rwanda in the early 1960s. It was later commonly used to refer to the RPF after it invaded Rwanda in 1990. During the genocide, this term was used by the interim authorities and RTLM to refer to the Tutsi generally.
Kangura	Literally "the voice which seeks to awaken and defend the 'majority people' [Hutu]". The Rwandan newspaper most notorious for hate speech against Tutsi. It was created in May 1990 by officials to counter the influence of the increasingly popular independent press, which experienced a boom in the late 1980s.
MDR	*Mouvement démocratique républicain* (Republican Democratic Movement). An opposition party which was established in

1991 and was named after the MDR-Parmehutu of President Grégoire Kayibanda.

MDR-Parmehutu

Mouvement démocratique républicain-Parti du mouvement de l'émancipation des Hutu (Republican Democratic Movement-Party of the Movement for the Emancipation of Hutu). Political party of President Grégoire Kayibanda, who ruled Rwanda from 1962-1973. This party emerged in the mid-1950s and had mainly Hutu members.

MRND

Mouvement révolutionnaire national du développement (National Revolutionary Movement for Development). The party was founded by President Juvénal Habyarimana in 1975. In 1991, the name was changed to the *Mouvement révolutionnaire national du développement et de la démocratie* (National Revolutionary Movement for Development and Democracy).

mwami

Traditional chief or king in Rwanda during the pre-colonial and colonial periods.

"Network Zero"

Death squad, which emerged in 1992 and was linked to members of the Presidential entourage. It is reported to have been responsible for assassinations of government critics from 1992-1994.

ORINFOR

A parastatal organization created by President Habyarimana in 1974 to control all the government media, including the two official newspapers, Radio Rwanda and Rwandan Television.

PDC

Parti démocrate chrétien (Christian Democratic Party). An opposition party in Rwanda.

PL

Parti libéral (Liberal Party). An opposition political party which was established in 1991.

préfecture

Region or province, the largest administrative division in Rwanda, which is headed by a *préfet* (Prefect) who is appointed by the President of the Republic. Rwanda is divided into 10 *préfectures*.

PSD

Parti social démocrate (Social Democratic Party). An opposition party which emerged in 1991.

Radio Muhabura

Literally means "leading the way". The radio station of the RPF which broadcast regularly out of Uganda, from mid-1992 until the end of the genocide.

RPA

Rwanda Patriotic Army. The armed wing of the RPF.

RPF

Rwanda Patriotic Front. A group of mainly Tutsi exiles based in Uganda who invaded Rwanda in October 1990. A cease-fire was later established in mid-1992. The RPF re-launched their offensive on 7 April 1994, after the genocide had begun, and won the war with the FAR in July 1994.

RTLM

Radio-Télévision Libre des Mille Collines (One Thousand Hills Free Radio). A radio station created in mid-1993 which was nominally independent but, like *Kangura*, had close connections to government officials and the security forces.

secteur	Sector, an administrative division in Rwanda. In every *commune* (see above), there are 7-10 *secteurs*, each of which is represented by an elected councillor.
Social Revolution	Movement in existence from 1959-1961 which led to the abolition of the Tutsi monarchy. The majority of Tutsi traditional leaders were killed or forced into exile. The Belgian colonial authorities, who supported this movement, replaced them with Hutu chiefs.
UNAMIR	United Nations Assistance Mission in Rwanda. An international force which was mandated by the United Nations Security Council in October 1993 to assist with the implementation of the Arusha Accords.
UNAR	*Union nationale rwandaise* (National Rwandan Union). Political party which emerged in the mid-1950s and mainly enjoyed support from Tutsi.

INTRODUCTION

The debate about "hate speech" has long been a vexing one for defenders of freedom of expression.[1] The same basic human rights instruments which guarantee the right to freedom of expression also prohibit advocacy of war and religious or racial hatred. Thus the ringing declaration of Article 19 of the International Covenant on Civil and Political Rights (ICCPR) in defence of freedom of expression is followed by the more sombre provisions of Article 20:

> 1 Any propaganda for war shall be prohibited by law.
> 2 Any advocacy of national, racial or religious hatred that constitutes incitement to discrimination, hostility or violence shall be prohibited by law.

In practice the interpretation of these words has been far from straight-forward. The difficulty lies in the phrase "that constitutes incitement". What is to be prohibited is not mere advocacy of unacceptable and dangerous views, but advocacy which may incite others to action. The freedom of expression community has tended to interpret this in the most liberal manner, taking the Voltairean view that defence of free speech only means anything if it entails defence of the right to express opinions which are generally considered obnoxious. Freedom of expression advocates have generally argued that restrictions on speech are more likely to be used against the defenders of oppressed groups, such as the victims of racism, rather than against racists. Apartheid South Africa, with its battery of laws preventing racial hate speech, was a prime example of this phenomenon. And the freedom of expression community has argued that the best antidote to hate speech is more speech — an extension of pluralism not its limitation. Thus incitement has been defined, according to the most liberal United States jurisprudence, to entail a test that there is a "clear and present danger" that the actions advocated will in fact be carried out.

Those defending the rights of oppressed communities, such as minority racial groups, have tended to take a different view. Yet, in most cases, the debate about "hate speech" has focused on the

1

propaganda of tiny extremist factions, such as racists and neo-Nazis, in well-established democracies.

And then came Rwanda. Almost the first thing that anyone noted about the genocide was the prominence of the media — notably the radio — among the advocates of hatred. It rapidly became the accepted wisdom to argue that the propaganda of Radio-Télévision Libre des Mille Collines (RTLM) was a principal cause of the genocide:

> Much of the responsibility for the genocide in Rwanda can be blamed on the media. Many people have heard of Radio des Mille Collines, which began broadcasting a steady stream of racist, anti-Tutsi invective in September 1993.
>
> ... it made sure that a large audience in Rwanda heard speeches by the likes of Léon Mugesera, who called on supporters of the Hutu regime to "dump the Tutsi in the Nyabarongo river".
>
> Radio des Mille Colline's shrill appeal for genocide on Rwandan airwaves accelerated as the apocalypse approached ... these calls became more intense as the bloodthirsty gangs carried out their sinister task.[2]

Various propositions flowed from this view, principally that actions should have been taken to silence RTLM. The inaction by the international community over RTLM became part of the general indictment of the failure of the Western powers and the United Nations (UN) system to prevent the genocide. Many observers, including human rights and freedom of expression groups, have since advocated a ban on "hate media" in other situations seen to be similar, above all in neighbouring Burundi.

Rwanda and Burundi are not the only recent instances of "hate radio" in Africa. In 1992 and 1993 the state-owned media in Zaire incited hatred against Kasaians and Balubas. Radio and television broadcasts accused people from Kasai Province of monopolizing the country's jobs and wealth. Half a million Kasaians were expelled from Shaba, many of whom later died in camps for the displaced.

In South Africa, Radio Pretoria and other far-right radio stations broadcast illegally in 1993 and 1994, defying somewhat half-hearted attempts by the Ministry of Home Affairs to close them by deploying armed and uniformed members of the neo-Nazi *Afrikaner Weerstandbeweging* (Afrikaner Resistance Movement) at the stations. This was in contrast to unlicensed community radio stations, such as Bush Radio on the Cape Flats which was closed down after a few hours on the air. The climax of the Radio Pretoria saga came in March 1994 when the station used its broadcasts to organize fascist commandos in defence of the "homeland" government of Lucas Mangope in Bophutatswana, which was threatened with a popular insurrection. An entire racial myth crumbled when the fascists were roundly defeated and the Mangope regime fell.

However, the role of RTLM in Rwanda remains, apparently, the clearest example of the baleful role that radio can play. Unlike Radio Pretoria, RTLM was directly, if covertly, linked to the government and benefited from that connection to enjoy a virtual radio monopoly (apart from the state-owned Radio Rwanda and Radio Muhabua, the pirate radio of the RPF). Many commentators have pointed out the crucial difference between hate speech emanating from weak and marginal groups with little power to carry out their threats and propaganda from official sources. The media in the former Yugoslavia had also played an important role in encouraging communal hostility and silencing conciliatory voices.[3] Yet, in its scale and apparent impact, hate radio in Rwanda seemed to have no parallel since the Nazi propaganda for genocide.

The purpose of this report, however, is to take none of this for granted. Most commentary on Rwandan hate radio has worked on the simple assumption that, since RTLM broadcast propaganda for genocide and genocide did indeed occur, there must be a causal relationship between the two. This is the same argument, in essence, as that propounded by those who argue that pornography is a prime cause of sexual deviancy or that film and television violence has led to an increase in violent crime. A detailed examination of these two propositions has shown that even where linkages can be established between media representations and social reality the causal relationship is obscure and almost impossible to establish with certainty. It might be argued that in the case of genocide the academic niceties of proving cause and effect should be dispensed with. Clearly the threat of genocide poses an urgency of response which will not allow for years or even months of academic reflection. But it does not remove the onus of proof from those who wish to ban media.

In the immediate aftermath of the genocide, many Western media accounts placed prime emphasis on the role of radio. Some of RTLM's alleged grisly pronouncements were often cited:

> The graves are still only half full! Help us to fill them! Form barriers! Block the infiltration of the cockroaches![4]

One journalists' organization argued that RTLM and the Hutu extremist newspaper *Kangura*

> ... prepared and accompanied the massacres. ... Their journalists are responsible, just like the killers of the government militias, for monstrous crimes which bloodied Rwanda. And, on these grounds, they must be held accountable".[5]

This was partly the characteristic narcissism of the media — a wish to believe in their own unbounded influence. More importantly, it perhaps reflected the interpretation of the genocide which prevailed in the contemporary accounts of outsiders: namely that it represented the unleashing of primordial hatreds between the two Rwandan "tribes". Subsequent analysis has done much to discredit that instant interpretation, revealing the genocide as a planned and highly organized event, in which moderate Hutu politicians were as much the target as Tutsi. Yet the role of the media in "inciting" the population has hardly been questioned. Investigation of the media role has not seriously tried to evaluate what RTLM and Radio Rwanda broadcast at different moments between 1990 and 1994 and what its impact was on the behaviour of the listeners. Journalists have been perhaps too willing to accept the perpetrators' own evaluation of the influences at work on them, as in this account given by a self-confessed member of the *Interahamwe* militia:[6]

> I did not believe that the Tutsi were coming to kill us ... but when the government radio continued to broadcast that they were coming to take our land, were coming to kill the Hutu — when this was broadcast over and over — I began to feel some kind of fear.[7]

Some accounts were truly bizarre. A Canadian journalist was quoted as saying:

> Hutus [*sic*] could be seen listening attentively to every broadcast. ... They held their cheap radios in one hand and machetes in the other, ready to start killing once the order had been given.[8]

According to the same account these radios were "Chinese-made receivers that were given to them freely and could only pick up RTLM".[9]

A much more serious case was presented by the human rights group African Rights:

> For the most part these journalists did not wield machetes or fire guns. Some of them did not even directly incite people to kill. But they all assisted in creating a climate of extremism and hysteria in which ordinary people could easily be influenced to become killers.[10]

The United Nations Special Rapporteur on Rwanda, Professor René Degni-Ségui, visited the country from 9 to 20 June 1994, while the genocide was still in progress. He concluded that the massacres seemed to have been planned. The campaign of "incitement to ethnic hatred and violence orchestrated by the media belonging to the government, or close to it, such as Radio Rwanda, and above all Radio-Télévision Libre des Mille Collines" pointed to this conclusion.[11] Professor

Degni-Ségui observed that broadcasting had been directed to different groups in different languages and with a different content. This was especially dangerous in relation to the illiterate rural population who only understood the information communicated in Kinyarwanda:[12]

> While broadcasts in French are inoffensive, those in Kinyarwanda are highly aggressive in tone. RTLM does not hesitate to call for the extermination of the Tutsi and it is notorious for the decisive role that it appears to have played in the massacres.[13]

This report does not claim to be a definitive study of the role of the radio in the Rwandan genocide, although it attempts to be a clear-sighted historical investigation without preconceptions. Its significance, however, is more than academic. Governments, political factions, international institutions and human rights groups have all tried to draw lessons from the role of radio in Rwanda in the hope of preventing a future genocide. Not surprisingly these lessons have been applied first to neighbouring Burundi, where the ethnic composition is similar even if the political balance is quite different. This makes it crucial that the lessons drawn are the correct ones.

Notes

[1] See, ARTICLE 19, *Striking a Balance: Hate Speech, Freedom of Expression and Non-discrimination* (London: May 1992).

[2] E Broadbent, "Media, even in the West, is partly to blame for the Rwandan Massacres", *The Gazette* (Montreal), 3 May 1995.

[3] See, ARTICLE 19, *Forging War: The Media in Serbia, Croatia and Bosnia-Hercegovina*, (London: May 1994).

[4] "Les fosses sont encore à moitié vides! Aidez-nous à les remplir! Formez des barrages! Bloquez les infiltrations des cancrelats!" F Misser, "Rwanda: médias et génocide", *Le Monde Diplomatique*, Aug. 1994.

[5] "... ont preparé et accompagné les massacres. ... Leurs journalistes sont responsables, au même titre que les tueurs des milices du pouvoir, des crimes

monstrueux qui ont ensanglanté le Rwanda. Et, à ce titre, ils doivent rendre des comptes". Reporters sans frontières, *Rwanda: médias de la haine ou presse démocratique?* (Paris: Sept. 1994).

[6] A militia affiliated with the *Mouvement révolutionnaire national pour le développement et la démocratie* (National Revolutionary Movement for Development and Democracy), established in 1992.

[7] B Berkeley, "Sounds of Violence: Rwanda's Killer Radio", *The New Republic*, 22-29 Aug. 1994.

[8] J Chilaizya, "Africa — Media Fuels Ethnic Strife — not only in Rwanda", Inter-Press Service, 12 May 1995.

[9] Ibid.

[10] African Rights, *Rwanda: Death, Despair and Defiance*, Revised Edition (London: 1995), 160.

[11] UN Doc. E/CN.4/1995/7, 28 June 1994, para. 26.

[12] See ARTICLE 19, *Protection of the Right to Information in Situations of Conflict and Tension: Submission to the Council of Europe Steering Committee on Mass Media* (London: ARTICLE 19, May 1995).

[13] Note 11 above, at para. 59.

POLITICAL BACKGROUND

1   History and Social Structure

Rwanda and Burundi have a similar history and social structure. In both countries the Hutu make up a substantial majority of the population — about 85 per cent — with the Tutsi comprising 14 per cent. The Twa constitute the remaining 1 per cent.

Conventional colonial historiography described the Hutu and Tutsi as different races, claiming that the Tutsi were a Nilo-Hamitic people, from the area now known as the Horn of Africa, and therefore were somehow more closely related to Europeans than other Africans. German, and later Belgian, officials maintained that the Tutsi were superior to the Hutu and, therefore, naturally better suited to serve as leaders.

Although these colonial theories have been disproved, there is still surprisingly little agreement about the origins and character of the different ethnic groups.[1] It is commonly accepted that the Twa or "pygmies" were the original inhabitants of the area, arriving between 2000 BC and 1000 AD, with a hunter-gatherer economy.

Between the fourth and seventh centuries AD, another group of clans settled in Rwanda and began farming the land. The nature of this second group remains the subject of ongoing debate by historians. One school of thought maintains that these settlers were baHutu (Hutu) and argues that the baTutsi (Tutsi) migrated to Rwanda much later, between the eleventh and twelfth centuries. Another group of historians refutes the notion that the Hutu and Tutsi ever had different geographical origins.[2] Instead, the latter school asserts that the second wave of settlers were banyaRwanda and that the distinctions between Hutu and Tutsi emerged from within the same society. It is believed that these categories may have been based on occupational differences, with the Hutu cultivating large areas of land and the Tutsi breeding livestock.

Regardless of the historical or geographic origins of the two groups, the categories of Hutu and Tutsi were already evident in Rwandan society by the early eighteenth century, when the territory known today as Rwanda comprised several small independent states.

8

Political Background

According to Catherine Newbury, these distinctions evolved with the emergence of a more centralized pre-colonial state in the mid-to-late nineteenth century. She argues:

> ... with the arrival of central authorities ... the categories of Hutu and Tutsi assumed new hierarchical overtones. ... Later, when the political arena widened and the intensity of political activity increased, these classifications became increasingly stratified and rigidified. More than simply conveying the connotation of cultural difference from Tutsi, Hutu identity came to be associated with and eventually defined by inferior status.[3]

These small states, which had existed since the fifteenth century, were united by the *Mwami* (traditional chief or king), Kigeri Rwabugiri, who ruled from 1860-1895. During this period, the *mwami*, as head of this highly centralized state, also became the symbol of political authority. As such he owned all the land and cattle and also acted as the supreme arbiter of justice in Rwanda. By the end of his rule, the Rwandan kingdom had become tightly organized into a series of administrative divisions which were mainly headed by Tutsi.[4] This unusually high level of administrative organization is still reflected in Rwanda today.[5]

The German colonization of the kingdoms of Rwanda and Burundi, which began in 1899, accentuated the divisions between Hutu and Tutsi. Although Rwanda and Burundi had formed separate pre-colonial states, Germany united them as one colony, Ruanda-Urundi. Unlike most areas in Africa then, the boundaries imposed by the colonial authorities largely corresponded to distinct pre-colonial political entities. Ruanda-Urundi was administered by only a small number of colonial authorities and they relied on the Tutsi traditional leaders already in place to enforce their rule. However, the colonial authorities formalized the previously fluid social distinctions between Hutu and Tutsi by introducing identity cards which classified the holder by ethnic origin. Each individual was assigned to the ethnicity of his or her father.[6]

As the colonial authorities sought to consolidate their power, they exacerbated tensions between Hutu and Tutsi by interfering with their traditional leadership structures. The German colonial authorities used the Tutsi *mwami* and other traditional Tutsi leaders to subject the entire territory to colonial rule. In northern Rwanda, where Hutu leaders had remained independent of the Tutsi-dominated pre-colonial state of *Mwami* Kigeri Rwabugiri, this policy caused widespread social strife, including a short-lived popular uprising in 1911, near Ruhengeri, which was suppressed by the German military.

When Belgium took over the colony of Ruanda-Urundi from Germany at the end of World War I, it continued to depend on Tutsi leaders to enforce its rule. In the late 1920s, the Belgian colonial authorities reorganized the system of traditional leaders and instituted a formal policy of replacing Hutu chiefs with Tutsi leaders throughout the country. By the 1930s, Tutsi leaders enjoyed a complete and unprecedented monopoly of "traditional" leadership positions in Rwanda.[7]

2   Revolution, Separation and Independence

Towards the mid-1950s, the policy of promoting Tutsi over Hutu as traditional leaders was challenged, as internal and external pressure mounted for the authorities to allow Hutu to participate in government. In 1945, Ruanda-Urundi had become a UN Trust Territory, with the effect that the UN required Belgium to steer the colony towards independence. In 1957 the UN sent a mission to Rwanda to evaluate the steps taken by the colonial authorities to promote democracy. Increasing national pressure to move towards more equal political representation before independence was articulated that same year in *The Manifesto of the Bahutu*, written by religious teacher and future President, Grégoire Kayibanda.

The Social Revolution of 1959-1961 was supported by both the colonial authorities and the Catholic missionaries, who were very influential in Rwandan society. Although its causes were more complex, the Revolution itself was sparked in November 1959 by an assault on a party official belonging to the *Mouvement démocratique républicain-Parti du mouvement de l'émancipation des Hutu*

(Republican Democratic Movement-Party of the Movement for the Emancipation of Hutu — MDR-Parmehutu) by a Tutsi. This incident led to an uprising in which the majority of the Tutsi chiefs (21 out of 43 chiefs and 314 out of 549 sub-chiefs) were killed or forced into exile. Hundreds of other Tutsi were massacred.[8] The colonial authorities replaced these leaders with Hutu chiefs, thereby abolishing the Tutsi monarchy.

During this period, several political parties emerged which were grouped along ethnic lines. The *Union nationale rwandaise* (National Rwandan Union — UNAR) and the *Rassemblement démocratique rwandais* (Rwandan Democratic Assembly — RADER) mainly enjoyed support from Tutsi communities, whereas the *Association pour la promotion sociale des masses* (Association for the Social Promotion of the Masses — APROSOMA) and the MDR-Parmehutu represented mostly Hutu constituents. This ethnic polarization of Rwandan politics became even more apparent with the legislative elections of September 1961, which were marred by widespread political violence against Tutsi. Hutu-dominated parties won 83 per cent of the votes nationwide, a figure which corresponded to the percentage of Hutu in the general population.[9] Rwanda and Burundi gained formal independence as separate states on 1 July 1962.

Under the First Republic of President Grégoire Kayibanda, which came to power in Rwanda after independence, the political system was monopolized by his Hutu-based MDR-Parmehutu, the only party to field candidates during the next legislative election in 1965. Meanwhile, President Kayibanda's government targeted both political opponents and Tutsi for intimidation and state-sponsored violence. This violence became more widespread when groups of Tutsi exiles based in Uganda and Burundi, who had fled the country during the Social Revolution, launched a series of attacks on Rwanda during the early 1960s. In Rwanda, the rebels were commonly referred to as *"Inyenzi"*, or "cockroaches", and the authorities responded to the attacks by retaliating against Tutsi living within the country. For example, in late 1963, following a major attack on the Bugesera region, government authorities organized massacres of Tutsi in many parts of the country. In the *préfecture* (province) of Gikongoro, some 5,000 to 8,000 Tutsi were killed — 10-20 per cent of the Tutsi population.[10]

3 From the First to the Second Republic

By the early 1970s, the Tutsi were so effectively excluded from political influence that politics began to divide along regional instead of ethnic lines. Hutu from northern Rwanda, particularly Ruhengeri and Gisenyi, began to resent the power and economic advantages enjoyed by the central region of Gitarama, President Kayibanda's home region.

In 1973, the authorities harassed and expelled Tutsi from schools, the civil service and private businesses. It is believed that these events were, in part, sparked off by the genocidal killings of Hutu in Burundi which had occurred in 1972. Hundreds were killed and this led to another major exodus of Tutsi from the country. Moreover, the persecution of Tutsi instigated more widespread violence in the country, fuelled by economic and regional resentments.[11]

In the midst of this social strife, the army, whose senior officers were mainly from the north, overthrew the Kayibanda government and General Juvénal Habyarimana, then Minister of Defence, became President.[12] General Habyarimana consolidated his authoritarian rule by proscribing the former ruling party and dissolving parliament. In 1974, a court martial sentenced President Kayibanda and seven other government members to death.[13] The next year President Habyarimana announced the creation of a new political party, the *Mouvement révolutionnaire national pour le développement* (National Revolutionary Movement for Development — MRND).

In 1978, President Habyarimana made the transition to civilian rule but retained the one-party system. In 1981 he reintroduced parliament, which was renamed the *Conseil national de développement* (National Council for Development — CND).[14] Moves towards economic nationalism were reversed, a more centralized system of administration was introduced, and government-sponsored political violence against Tutsi largely abated in the absence of border incursions. Despite this, widespread discrimination against the minority continued.

4 The Early 1990s: Transition to Democracy and War with the RPF

On 1 October 1990, the Rwanda Patriotic Army (RPA), the armed wing of the Rwanda Patriotic Front (RPF), a group of mainly Tutsi exiles based in Uganda, invaded Rwanda. The RPA initially numbered approximately 2,500, many of whom had previously fought in Yoweri Museveni's National Resistance Army (NRA) which overthrew Uganda's President Obote in January 1986. The RPA increased its strength to approximately 7,000 at the height of the war.[15]

The RPF leaders described their invasion as an attempt to secure the right of return for Rwandan exiles who had been forced to flee the country since the Social Revolution. Although, theoretically, the exiles had been allowed to return under Grégoire Kayibanda's government, during the Second Republic the government maintained that the country was too overpopulated to accommodate them.[16] At the time of the invasion, Rwandan Tutsi exiles were estimated at 600,000, nearly 9 per cent of the population within the country.[17]

The RPF claimed that the attack was the sole means of pressuring President Habyarimana's government to allow democratic change. However, one week earlier, the Rwandan government, under internal and foreign pressure since the late 1980s to address the question of a democratic transition, had begun to take steps in this direction. On 24 September 1990, a *commission nationale de synthèse* (National Commission of Synthesis) was created to draft a *charte politique nationale* (National Political Charter) which would establish regulations governing the formation of other political groupings.[18] Although the Commission suspended its work for one month following the RPF invasion, by the end of the year it had published its findings, a draft *charte politique nationale* as well as "a draft constitution and bill on the [formation of] political parties".[19]

By early 1991, the government was under great pressure to allow multi-party politics. In March, political groupings which had previously operated clandestinely began to publicly demand formal recognition and to be allowed to participate in government. The newspaper *Le Démocrate* published a letter signed by 237 persons, many of whom were from Gitarama *préfecture*, who declared their intention to organize a political party called the *Mouvement démocratique républicain* (Republican Democratic Movement — MDR), named after Grégoire Kayibanda's MDR-Parmehutu. Other political interest groups, the *Parti social démocrate* (Social Democratic Party — PSD), the *Parti libéral* (Liberal Party — PL) and the *Parti démocrate chrétien* (Christian Democratic Party — PDC) also became active.[20] The following month the ruling party changed its name from the *Mouvement révolutionnaire national du développement* (National Revolutionary Movement for Development — MRND) to the *Mouvement révolutionnaire national du développement et de la démocratie* (National Revolutionary Movement for Development and Democracy — MRND), ostensibly to demonstrate its support for the process of political reform. In June, the 1978 Constitution was amended to abolish the one-party form of government. This was followed by the enactment of the Political Parties Law, which legalized opposition parties, five of which were officially registered the following month.

In late 1991, the government engaged in negotiations with leaders of several opposition parties on the possibility of adopting a transitional coalition government in which the major opposition groups would be represented. Initial discussions failed to produce an agreement by the end of the year and, on 30 December 1991, the Prime Minister designate formed a new government with only one minister from an opposition party, the PDC.

A transitional coalition government which represented several major opposition parties was finally established in April 1992. President Habyarimana appointed as Prime Minister MDR representative Dismas Nsengiyaremye, who formed a government with three other opposition parties, the PSD, the PL, and PDC. The MRND retained half of the cabinet posts whilst the remainder were divided amongst the four opposition parties. Executive power was shared between the President and the Prime Minister. It was this government that initiated negotiations with the RPF which ultimately led to a cease-fire and peace accord.

On 24 May 1992, Foreign Minister Boniface Ngulinzira met with RPF Vice-Chairman Patrick Mazimpaka. A delegation from the MDR, PSD and PL then organized meetings with RPF leaders in Brussels (Belgium) on 6 June. The following day, the RPF declared that it would cease hostilities and undertook to use only political means to pursue its agenda with the Rwandan government. On 12 July, the RPF and the Rwandan government signed a cease-fire and began negotiations over a peace agreement.[21]

Although the RPF broke the cease-fire on 8 February 1993, leading to a massive increase in the number of internally displaced people, from 300,000 (1990-1992) to 860,000 by early March, a cease-fire was enacted the following month and negotiations aimed at a peace agreement continued.[22] The Arusha Accords, which defined the terms of the peace agreement with the RPF, were signed in August 1993, and were originally scheduled to be implemented by late 1993. However, the implementation of the Accords was repeatedly obstructed by President Habyarimana and other MRND politicians, and still had not been effected when Juvénal Habyarimana's plane was shot down on 6 April 1994.

The Arusha Accords were designed to change the political system from a presidential to a parliamentary one, with most of the President's responsibilities assumed by a Council of Ministers. In the interim period, cabinet positions in the Council of Ministers of a Broad-based Transitional Government (BBTG) would be shared between the MRND, internal opposition parties and the RPF. The MRND would retain only 5 out of 19 positions. In addition, a transitional National Assembly would be established with representatives from these parties. Furthermore, the Accords called for the integration of the RPA into the *Forces Armées Rwandaises* (Rwandan Armed Forces — FAR) on a 40-60 per cent basis, which necessitated a significant demobilization of government troops. During the transitional period, it was agreed that the RPF would maintain a battalion of 600 troops in Kigali, stationed in the parliament building, the CND, to provide further security for RPF leaders. Another RPF battalion remained stationed in northern Rwanda. In October 1993, the UN Security Council passed Resolution 872 which approved an international force of 2,500 troops, UNAMIR (UN Assistance Mission in Rwanda), to assist in the implementation of the Accords and the integration of the two armies. The first of these troops were stationed in Rwanda by late October.[23]

5 Orchestrating Violence: The Growth of MRND and CDR Militias

The process of democratization and the Arusha Accords represented a major threat to members of the ruling elite. In particular, the reforms in the military and government dealt a blow to hardline sections of the FAR and the MRND. President Habyarimana had publicly expressed his ambiguous attitude towards the Arusha negotiations as early as 15 November 1992 in a speech where he described the Accords as "scraps of paper", suggesting they could easily be disregarded.[24]

In 1992, just as the multi-party transitional coalition government began to institute a series of reforms, the ruling party founded a militia, the *Interahamwe*, meaning, "Those who work together". Simultaneously, another extremist political party emerged, the *Coalition pour la défense de la république* (Coalition for the Defence of the Republic — CDR), which also organized a militia called the *Impuzamugambi* or "Those with a single purpose".[25] Although sometimes described as random groups of young thugs, the *Interahamwe* and the *Impuzamugambi* were centrally organized, with a national president, vice-president, and leaders down to the neighbourhood level. Party leaders recruited militia members from the party youth organizations, paid them and provided them with military training, weapons and sometimes uniforms. These groups began to gradually expand throughout the country during 1992, setting up roadblocks in various areas, to stop and harass individuals. They were first reported to have played a role in the government-sponsored violence during the Bugesera massacre in March 1992.

The UN Special Rapporteur on Extrajudicial, Summary or Arbitrary Executions, Bacre Waly Ndiaye, reported that in April 1993 both militias were "guilty of incitement to ethnic violence against the Tutsi, massacres of the civilian populations and political assassinations".[26] He also noted that the militias were widely believed to represent attempts by "certain authorities to 'privatize' violence by channelling it through such groups, so as to avoid being held responsible for the massacres".[27]

Although opposition members of the coalition transitional government publicly condemned the militia violence, both groups are reported to have received strong backing from MRND officials and members of the security forces. Human Rights Watch reported that in late 1993 and early 1994, militia members were given rigorous military training in a military camp in the north-eastern region of Mutara.[28]

In addition to the militias, another clandestine organization with official backing emerged in 1992. A death squad, "Network Zero", is reported to have targeted political opponents for assassination, "thus discrediting democratic reforms, the multi-party system and the peace process initiated at Arusha".[29] The leading members of "Network Zero" were prominent figures in the presidential entourage, known as *Akazu* ("the little house"), including President Habyarimana's three brothers-in-law, Colonel Elie Sagatwa, the President's personal secretary, Séraphin Rwabukumba, and Protais Zigiranyirazo; Alphonse Ntirivamunda, Director-General in the Ministry of Public Works and son-in-law of President Habyarimana, Captain Pascal Simbikangwa, Côme Bizimungu and Charles Nzabagerageza, former *préfets* of Gisenyi and Ruhengeri.[30]

Clearly, in 1992, there were already signs that the clandestine organizations were centrally organized and highly structured. Human Rights Watch reported, in February 1992, that "most leading activists [in Rwanda] believe that the government has compiled lists naming people to be assassinated when circumstances require. People in smaller cities and towns, as well as leaders in the capital, assume that such lists exist".[31] Jean Birara, former governor of the Central Bank and relative of General Déogratias Nsabimana[32], reported to the Belgian press that by April 1993, these militias had prepared a list of 500 people targeted for killing. He claimed that this list had grown to include 1,500 individuals in the Kigali area by February 1994.[33]

The existence of such lists became more evident in the months leading up to the genocide. In January 1994, General Dallaire, head of the UNAMIR contingent in Rwanda, reported to the UN Security Council that he had evidence that lists had been drawn up of Tutsi to be exterminated.[34] Moreover, this period was marked by a visible increase in the activities of the paramilitary groups. The US State Department report for 1994 noted that in January and February 1994 "government militiamen killed several dozen civilians, blocked streets, searched cars, beat perceived opposition supporters and damaged property".[35] The violence by MRND and CDR militias during this period was also a major factor in stalling the implementation of the Arusha Accords. In January and February, UNAMIR intervened to block the importation of several unauthorized planeloads of arms at Kigali airport, destined for the Rwandan armed forces.[36]

6 The Genocide

On 6 April 1994, around 8.30 p.m., the plane carrying President Juvénal Habyarimana and President of Burundi Cyprien Ntaryamira was targeted by a ground-to-air missile and exploded just as it was nearing the airport in Kigali. All on board were instantly killed. The two Presidents had been returning from a meeting of regional heads of state in Dar-es-Salaam in which Juvénal Habyarimana had finally agreed to implement the Arusha Accords of August 1993. Within half an hour of the crash and before any public announcement was made, government security forces and militias threw up roadblocks in Kigali and began selective killing.[37] It has not been possible to establish who was responsible for downing the plane. However, many observers believe that the speed with which the government armed forces started the bloodshed would suggest that both the crash and the violence which followed were part of a highly organized plan. What happened over the next 24 hours has been described as "the almost simultaneous occurrence of a military coup, renewed civil war, systematic political assassinations, and commencement of genocide".[38]

Within the first week, an estimated 20,000 people were killed in the Kigali area alone. In less than three months, approximately 500,000 were slaughtered; two million became refugees; and one million were internally displaced.[39] French historian Gérard Prunier estimates that 80 per cent of the victims were killed during the first six weeks of the genocide, an extermination rate which would prove five times as fast as that of the Nazi death camps.[40]

The earliest victims were cabinet members and politicians from opposition parties as well as leaders of civil society. Prime Minister Agathe Uwilingiyimana was killed along with her husband by government forces early in the morning of 7 April. Ten Belgian peacekeepers assigned to guard her were disarmed, taken to a military camp, and killed. Minister of Agriculture Frédéric Nzamurambaho, from the PSD, and Minister of Labour and Social Affairs Landoald Ndasingwa, PL leader and a Tutsi, were both slaughtered on 7 April. President of the Supreme Court Joseph Kavaruganda and Minister of Information Faustin Rucogoza, who had tried to introduce reform at Radio Rwanda, were also among the first to be killed. Scores of independent journalists and human rights activists were hunted down and killed within the next number of days.

A self-proclaimed "interim government" was formed on 8 April, by which time all the opposition cabinet members had been killed or forced into hiding. Théodore Sindikubwabo, President of the CND, was sworn in as President, citing Article 42 of the 1991 Constitution. This was inconsistent with the Arusha Accords, however, which required that if the President were deceased or became incapacitated, a new head of state would be elected during a special joint session of the BBTG and the transitional National Assembly.[41] Although it claimed to follow the protocol of 7 April 1992, which had established the first transitional government with opposition representation, this self-proclaimed cabinet drew all its members from the MRND, the CDR and the extremist "Hutu Power" factions of several opposition parties which had been close to the MRND.[42]

The RPF responded early in the morning of 7 April 1994 by launching a military offensive from northern Rwanda, where most of its troops had been stationed. Later that day, RPF forces arrived in Kigali to reinforce the 600 RPA troops stationed in the parliament building in accordance with the peace agreement.[43] On 12 April, as a result of fighting between the RPA and the FAR in the capital, the interim government moved from Kigali to Gitarama. By mid-June, the RPF advance had forced the interim government to relocate to Gisenyi *préfecture*. Although the genocide was clearly distinct from the combat, UN officials, including UN Special Representatives, Secretary-General Jacques Roger Booh-Booh and, later, Shaharyar Khan, failed to recognize this and instead lobbied the RPF and the FAR for a cease-fire. However, the RPF refused to consider a cease-fire while government forces continued the massacres of civilians.[44]

The international community failed to take any effective action to stop the widespread killings during the genocide. The only foreign military intervention during this period was *Opération Turquoise*, which the French military began on 23 June 1994. Although primarily a humanitarian mission, *Opération Turquoise* established several "safe havens" in south-west Rwanda which protected an estimated 12-15,000 Tutsi from slaughter. Meanwhile, the UN not only failed to respond to the crisis; on 21 April the UN Security Council cut the size of the UNAMIR force from 2,500 to 270 troops. On 8 June the Security Council passed another resolution authorizing the use of 5,000 UNAMIR troops with a stronger mandate. This step proved futile as the necessary logistical support for this mission was not forthcoming from the United States (US) until late July. By that point the genocide had already ended with the RPF victory of 18 July. The next day, Pasteur Bizimungu became President and Major General Paul Kagame was appointed Vice-President and Defence Minister.[45]

Notes

[1] The Hutu and Tutsi are considered to constitute distinct ethnic groups, although they speak Kinyarwanda in Rwanda and Kirundi in Burundi and share a common culture.

[2] The Economist Intelligence Unit, *Country Profile, Rwanda, Burundi: Historical background, 1995-96* (London: EIU, 1995), 4.

[3] C Newbury, *The cohesion of oppression. Clientship and ethnicity in Rwanda 1860-1960*, in: Joint Evaluation of Emergency Assistance to Rwanda, *The International Response to Conflict and Genocide: Lessons from the Rwanda Experience, (Study 1: Historical Perspective: Some Explanatory Factors)*, (Denmark: Steering Committee of the Joint Evaluation of Emergency Assistance to Rwanda, March 1996), 23.

[4] Joint Evaluation of Emergency Assistance to Rwanda, note 3 above.

[5] Rwanda is composed of 10 *préfectures* (provinces), each headed by a *préfet* (prefect) who is appointed by the President of the Republic. Each *préfecture* comprises 143 *communes* (municipalities), which are all led by a *bourgemestre* (mayor), who is also appointed by the President. (Ibid., at 15). Each *commune* is organized into 7-10 *secteurs* (sectors) which are each represented by an elected councillor. In turn, every sector is divided into *cellules* (cells),

which are headed by an elected committee of five people. The committees choose a *responsable de cellule* (cell leader) to represent them. Fédération internationale des droits de l'homme, Africa Watch, Union interafricaine des droits de l'homme et des peuples, Centre international des droits de la personne et du développement démocratique, *Report of the International Commission of Investigation on Human Rights Violations in Rwanda Since October 1, 1990 (January 7-21, 1993) Final Report* (New York: Human Rights Watch/Africa, March 1993), 12.

[6] Identity cards indicating ethnicity were retained by the First and Second Republics in the post-independence period, however, they have since been abolished by the Rwanda Patriotic Front, which took power on 19 July 1994.

[7] F Reyntjens, *L'Afrique des Grands Lacs en crise: Rwanda, Burundi: 1988-1994* (Paris: Éditions Karthala, 1994), 20.

[8] Ibid., at 27.

[9] Ibid.

[10] Ibid.

[11] Joint Evaluation of Emergency Assistance to Rwanda, note 3 above, at 32.

[12] Habyarimana retained both positions until the first transitional government of Prime Minister Sylvestre Nsanzimana of Dec. 1991.

[13] Some of the government members were granted clemency which reduced the death sentences to prison terms. Grégoire Kayibanda was placed under house arrest but died two years later after being refused access to medical care.

[14] The Economist Intelligence Unit, note 2 above, at 6.

[15] Joint Evaluation of Emergency Assistance to Rwanda, note 4 above, at 35.

[16] Reyntjens, note 7 above, at 143.

[17] Ibid., at 25.

[18] Ibid., at 104.

[19] Ibid., at 105.

[20] Ibid., at 106.

[21] Joint Evaluation of Emergency Assistance to Rwanda, *The International Response to Conflict and Genocide: Lessons from the Rwanda Experience (Study 2: Early Warning and Conflict Management)* (Denmark: Steering Committee of the Joint Evaluation of Emergency Assistance to Rwanda, March 1996), 24.

[22] G Prunier, *The Rwanda Crisis 1959-1994: History of a Genocide* (London and New York: Hurst & Company and Columbia University Press, 1995), 174.

[23] Joint Evaluation of Emergency Assistance to Rwanda, note 3 above, at 46.

[24] "Chiffons de papier", in Reyntjens, note 7 above, at 205.

[25] Although originally an opposition party, in late 1993 the CDR formed an alliance with extremists in the MRND.

[26] UN Economic and Social Council, *Extrajudicial, Summary or Arbitrary Executions, Addendum — Report by Mr B W Ndiaye, Special Rapporteur, on his mission to Rwanda from 8 to 17 April 1993*, UN Doc. E/CN.4/1994/7/Add.1., dated 11 Aug. 1993, 12.

[27] Ibid.

[28] Human Rights Watch/Africa, *Genocide in Rwanda: April-May 1994* (New York: May 1994), 2.

[29] UN Economic and Social Council, note 26 above, at 13.

[30] Prunier, note 22 above, at 168.

[31] Africa Watch, *Rwanda: Talking Peace and Waging War: Human Rights Since the October 1990 Invasion* (New York: Africa Watch, 27 Feb. 1992), 24.

[32] Chief of Staff of the Armed Forces until killed in the plane crash with President Habyarimana on 6 April 1994.

[33] Prunier, note 22 above, at 222.

[34] This cable is reproduced in F Reyntjens, *Rwanda: Trois jours qui ont fait basculer l'histoire, Cahiers Africaine no. 16* (Institut-Africain-CEDAF and l'Harmattan: Brussels and Paris, 1995). It cites a report from an informant that the *Interahamwe* could kill up to 1,000 Tutsi in 20 minutes.

[35] US Department of State, *Country Reports on Human Rights Practices for 1994* (Washington: US Government Printing Office, 1995), 200-208.

[36] Human Rights Watch/Africa, note 28 above, at 2.

[37] US Department of State, note 35 above.

[38] Joint Evaluation of Emergency Assistance to Rwanda, note 21 above, at 41. For an analysis of the plane crash and events during the first several days of the genocide, see Reyntjens, note 34 above.

[39] Joint Evaluation of Emergency Assistance to Rwanda, note 3 above, at 50.

[40] Prunier, note 22 above, at 261. The exact death toll will probably never be known. Most observers estimate the deaths by genocide at 500,000, however, Prunier has put forward the higher figure of 800,000, which he bases on demographic calculations. Professor Filip Reyntjens has estimated that the total number of deaths caused by the genocide, war and refugee crisis from April to the end of September 1994 was 1.3 million.

[41] This provision of the Accords technically was effective from 4 Aug. 1993, however, by April 1994 the transitional institutions it referred to still had not been put into place. Reyntjens, note 7 above, at 297.

[42] Reyntjens, note 34 above, at 90. These factions had caused splits within most of the opposition parties by late 1993.

[43] Ibid. It was widely reported in the international media that the RPF launch began on 8 April 1994.

[44] Joint Evaluation of Emergency Assistance to Rwanda, note 3 above, at 54.

The RPA also killed scores of civilians. Amnesty International has reported that possibly thousands of unarmed civilians are believed to have been summarily executed by the RPA from April-July 1994. However, more precise figures are unavailable. See, Amnesty International, *Rwanda: Reports of Killings and Abductions by the Rwandese Patriotic Army, April-August 1994* (London: Amnesty International, Oct. 1994).

[45] Ibid., at 78-80.

Chapter 1

OCTOBER 1990: War of Propaganda and Misinformation

When the Rwanda Patriotic Front (RPF) invaded Rwanda from Uganda on 1 October 1990, the Rwandan government responded with more than a military defence. It launched a propaganda war against the RPF in an attempt to discredit the rebels and exaggerate the military threat which they represented. At the onset of the war, the Rwanda Patriotic Army (RPA) consisted of approximately 2,500 soldiers, mostly Tutsi exiles from Rwanda, many of whom had recently deserted from Ugandan President Museveni's National Resistance Army.[1] Rwandan officials, however, repeatedly overstated the size of the force and claimed that the invasion was the work not only of Rwandan rebels but also of the entire Ugandan army. On 8 October 1990, Foreign Minister Casimir Bizimungu (later Minister of Health under the interim government of April 1994) claimed that the RPA numbered "10,000; a figure which can double or triple if recruitment from the Ugandan army continues — and there is abundant evidence on this matter".[2]

Meanwhile, the RPF leaders skilfully presented their own explanation of the attack to the international media and maintained they were fighting President Habyarimana's government because it systematically violated basic human rights and refused hundreds of thousands of Rwandan refugees the right to return. The RPF claimed that it intended to establish a democratic government in Rwanda which would eliminate ethnic and regional discrimination.

A large section of the international press accepted this version of events without question, despite the fact that the government had already begun tentative steps to allow a democratic transition and an organized repatriation of the hundreds of thousands of refugees in Uganda. The RPF propaganda was so well received internationally that several non-governmental organizations and regional specialists in Belgium were prompted to jointly publish an article on 16 October, "Une colère de temps de guerre au Rwanda" ("Wartime Anger in

Rwanda"), which refutes the RPF's depiction of its invasion and strongly condemns the attack.[3]

Within the country, however, the government interpretation of the invasion prevailed and the RPF, labelled by the authorities *"Inyenzi"*, was accused of trying to re-establish the Tutsi monarchy in order to oppress the "Hutu majority". Then Foreign Minister Casimir Bizimungu warned: "this terrorist organization has as its only aim the establishment of a minority regime embodying feudalism with a modern outlook. The Rwandan people will not agree to reverse history, leading the nation's dynamic forces back to feudal drudgery and enslavement".[4] This is a common reference, however distorted, to the supposed domination of the Hutu by Tutsi traditional leaders throughout the pre-colonial and colonial periods. The Social Revolution of 1959-1961, which abolished the Tutsi monarchy, had been used since Independence as a rallying point for the Rwandan government, a symbol of freedom of the majority from oppression by a tyrannical minority.[5]

The authorities identified the RPF with the Tutsi leaders of the colonial era, associating them with a repressive past, in part, because of the large numbers of Tutsi soldiers within their ranks. Similarly, the Rwandan government accused Tutsi civilians from the interior of supporting the RPF by virtue of their ethnicity and, within days of the attack, began indiscriminately to round up and detain Tutsi throughout the country. According to the UN Special Rapporteur on Extrajudicial, Summary or Arbitrary Executions, Bacre Waly Ndiaye:

> The result of this attack and of a policy of deliber-
> ately-targeted government propaganda was that all
> Tutsi inside the country were collectively labelled
> accomplices of the RPF.[6]

1 Military Theatrics: The Fake Attack on Kigali (4-5 October)

For the Rwandan government, the propaganda war soon escalated beyond rhetoric. During the night of 4-5 October 1990, the Rwandan authorities simulated what they claimed was an RPA attack on Kigali, by using the FAR who fired guns within the capital from 1.00 a.m. until 7.00 a.m. Although the shooting caused no casualties and only minimal destruction in Kigali, government officials and Radio Rwanda convincingly reported that the city had been the target of an RPA onslaught, and some reports even claimed that corpses of rebels had been found in the capital. This explanation of events was relayed by most of the international media, including the *New York Times* and several wire services.[7]

The government used the fake attack to heighten fears about the RPF and the war itself, suggesting that the hostilities had quickly spread from the Ugandan border to the more densely populated Rwandan capital. The simulated attack was also used by the Rwandan government to lobby France, Belgium and Zaire for further military intervention in support of the FAR.[8] A few days later, the French government increased the size of its military contingent in Rwanda from 150 to 600 soldiers.

More importantly, the staged incursion served as a pretext for the authorities to step up the arrests of Tutsi and government critics, whom they categorically accused of working for the RPF. By mid-October, between 6,000 and 7,000 persons were detained throughout the country, approximately half of whom were arrested in Kigali and about 90 per cent of whom were Tutsi. Nor did the authorities deny that they were targeting Tutsi civilians. In a speech on 15 October, President Habyarimana explained why so many Tutsi intellectuals had been arrested, stating that the Minister of Justice, Théoneste Mujyanama, "has decided that these [Tutsi] are accomplices. In order to prepare an attack of such a scale, there needed to be people who could be trusted. Rwandans of the same ethnic group were the obvious choice".[9] In late November, before any of the accused were brought to trial, the Minister of Justice claimed to have irrefutable proof that all the accused were guilty.[10]

After a series of trials in January 1991, dozens were sentenced to imprisonment and a few received death sentences. When the more independent Sylvestre Nsanzimana was appointed Minister of Justice in February, however, he ordered the immediate release of 3,500 detainees on the ground that there was no evidence against them.[11]

Meanwhile, the lull which followed the staged invasion and the massive arrests was presented by the government as proof of its success in responding to a dangerous rebel group. On 15 October 1990, in a speech broadcast by Radio Rwanda, President Habyarimana announced:

> On the military front ... the infiltration of assail-
> ants and rebels into [*sic*] the Kigali *préfecture* is at
> the present hour under control. Enemy arms caches
> in the capital and in the environs have been seized
> and, above all, the majority of the infiltrators have
> been spotted. ...[12]

Despite this professed confidence in the ability of the Rwandan armed forces to repulse the guerrilla movement, President Habyarimana used the fake attack as a pretext to call upon civilians to participate in the defence of the nation. Presenting what amounted to typical wartime propaganda, he cautioned citizens about the dangers of the forces pitted against them and asked people to be wary and watchful. He also warned:

> The situation seems to be under control, but the
> enemy being what he is, we must remain extremely
> vigilant, not only during the coming days but also
> during the coming weeks and months.

These calls for vigilance were followed by repeated requests by the President for people to assist the armed forces in the battle against the RPF.

In an earlier speech on 11 October, he had claimed that the rebels were disguising themselves as civilians and asked people to denounce all possible infiltrators to the FAR.[13] On 2 November, President Habyarimana again claimed that the RPA troops, disguised as farmers and herders, were preparing a "surprise attack", and stated: "do not hesitate to arrest any suspect and bring them to the relevant authorities".[14]

With international criticism mounting over the arbitrary detentions of Tutsi and government critics, in a broadcast on Radio Rwanda, President Habyarimana urged citizens not to believe reports by the international media on events in Rwanda and warned:

The aggression against our country is not just military. It is also one which manipulated the international media with disinformation about [the] truth of the Rwandan position ... we have also been surprised by the strength of the manipulation — planned as we know now, planned for a long time — of some Western media — and important media at that — which aimed at turning world opinion against our country. Our country accordingly was and remains the target of attacks and lies, of systematic lies which we can only describe as diabolic.[15]

According to President Habyarimana, the criticism by the international media represented yet another aspect of the RPF invasion. He argued that "disinformation" about Rwanda in the foreign press was not the result of a genuine lack of understanding by foreign journalists of events in Rwanda or of the reasons behind the RPF attack. Rather, critical reports were a premeditated plot, conceived by the foreign press corps together with the RPF to further destabilize, vilify and isolate a country while subjecting it to armed guerrilla incursions.

2   Radio Rwanda and the Rwanda Patriotic Front

Radio Rwanda was the main source of information on the war for the vast majority of Rwandans and, for many, it was the only medium they had access to, given the high illiteracy level and the small percentage of the population which could understand programmes in French or English on international radio stations. The accuracy and the neutrality of Radio Rwanda's reporting of the war varied at different points throughout the war, often according to the level of tension surrounding military and political developments.

On several occasions, Radio Rwanda provided patently false and inflammatory reports on the RPF and the extent of the hostilities. A series of broadcasts from 1990 to 1992 depicted the RPF as a satanic group which waged war solely through attacks on civilians. A report on 22 November 1990 warned listeners, "since their goal is to exterminate and enslave us, we must not feel any mercy towards them".[16] Although there was no evidence of mass executions of civilians by the RPF before February 1993, several broadcasts by Radio Rwanda in late 1990 claimed that the RPA soldiers beat and killed everyone in their path, including children and Ugandan citizens. Continuing this wartime propaganda, in late November 1990, Radio Rwanda reported: "Their methods remain the same: massacres, rapes and looting".[17] Another report stated that "rebels have committed inhuman acts that have struck both the administration and the army with awe".[18] Other broadcasts accused the RPF of using witchcraft to support their military offensive.[19]

After the appointment in December 1990 of Ferdinand Nahimana as Director of the *Office Rwandais d'Information* (the Rwandan Office of Information — ORINFOR)[20], the radio broadcasts tended to become more virulent and distorted. In late January 1991, the RPF captured Ruhengeri town for one day and liberated prisoners from the state prison before retreating. Ferdinand Nahimana gave Radio France Internationale a creative account of the incursion, stating: "these attackers included a number of Libyan commandos ... the proof comes from the information we received precisely from those who fled Ruhengeri prison, who say that Arabs had freed them".[21] A few days later, Radio Rwanda cited a witness who claimed that the RPF force which liberated the prison was composed of "entirely ... suicidal and drugged people, who invaded ... in their hundreds but who left behind hundreds of dead". A report several months later claimed that RPA soldiers "have an unparalleled instinct for killing".[22]

Although the guerrilla war continued at a low level of intensity throughout 1991, Radio Rwanda repeated, over several months, that thousands more rebels and Ugandans were in the process of massing on the border and that a large invasion was imminent. While it exaggerated the threat posed by the rebels, Radio Rwanda generally denied that any losses had been incurred by the Rwandan army. After May 1992, the rebels occupied a small portion of Rwandan territory in the north, a fact which the station continually denied. In addition, it frequently broadcast false information about RPF leaders and on 12 February 1992 claimed that RPF leader Paul Kagame (Rwanda's current Vice-President and Minister of Defence) had been killed by a mine.

Notes

[1] G Prunier, *The Rwanda Crisis 1959-1994: History of a Genocide* (London and New York: Hurst & Company and Columbia University Press, 1995), 93.

[2] Radio Rwanda (French), 1800 GMT, 8 Oct. 1990, *BBC Summary of World Broadcasts*.

[3] F Reyntjens, *L'Afrique des Grands Lacs en crise: Rwanda, Burundi: 1988-1994* (Paris: Éditions Karthala, 1994), 102.

[4] Radio Rwanda, 8 Oct. 1990, *BBC Summary of World Broadcasts*.

[5] The widespread violence against Tutsi during this period, as well as the role and responsibility of the colonial authorities in exploiting the Tutsi monarchy, were systematically omitted from this official and revisionist account of the history of the Rwandan Republic.

[6] UN Economic and Social Council, *Extrajudicial, Summary or Arbitrary Executions, Addendum — Report by Mr B W Ndiaye, Special Rapporteur, on his mission to Rwanda from 8 to 17 April 1993*, UN Doc. E/CN.4/1994/7/Add.1., dated 11 Aug. 1993, 12.

[7] Fédération internationale des droits de l'homme, Africa Watch, Union interafricaine des droits de l'homme et des peuples, Centre internationale des droits de la personne et du développement démocratique, *Report of the International Commission of Investigation on Human Rights Violations in Rwanda Since October 1, 1990 (January 7-21, 1993) Final Report* (New York: Human Rights Watch/Africa, March 1993), 6.

[8] On 4 Oct., France and Belgium agreed to send troops on a "humanitarian mission" and Zaire sent a contingent of 500 soldiers, who participated directly in the fighting. Reyntjens, note 3 above, at 93.

[9] "A jugé que ces derniers sont complices. Car ... pour préparer une attaque de telle envergure, il fallait qu'il y ait des gens de confiance. Les Rwandais de la même ethnie offrent mieux cette possibilité". Reyntjens, note 3 above, at 94.

[10] Ibid., at 96.

[11] In April 1991, a Presidential decree commuted all the death sentences which had been issued. Following their release, many of the former accused

continued to face harassment by the authorities; for example, some were removed from their positions of employment and others had their passports confiscated. Ibid., at 98.

[12] "Rwandan President on Current Situation; Castigates Media 'Disinformation'", excerpts from recording of speech by Juvénal Habyarimana, 15 Oct. 1990, *BBC Summary of World Broadcasts.*

[13] "Communiqué from the Minister of National Defence following the attack ... on 1 October ... and in Kigali in the night of 4-5 October 1990," Radio Rwanda, 1800 GMT, 11 Oct. 1990, *BBC Summary of World Broadcasts*, 13 Oct. 1990.

[14] "Rwandan government communiqué hails victory but calls for vigilance", Radio Rwanda, Kigali (French), 1800 GMT, 2 Nov. 1990, *BBC Summary of World Broadcasts*, 5 Nov. 1990.

[15] *BBC Summary of World Broadcasts*, note 12 above.

[16] Radio Rwanda, Kigali (French), 1800 GMT, 22 Nov. 1990, *BBC Summary of World Broadcasts*, 24 Nov. 1990.

[17] Radio Rwanda, Kigali (French), 1115 GMT, 27 Nov. 1990, *BBC Summary of World Broadcasts*, 29 Nov. 1990.

[18] As quoted in Reuters, "Rwandan Radio Reports Rebel Atrocities in Renewed Fighting," 6 Nov. 1990.

[19] Reuters, 23 Dec. 1990. Creative and sometimes fantastic portrayals of the RPF troops occasionally made an impression on people in rural areas. Alain Destexthe writes that some peasants were surprised when they first saw RPF soldiers, as they literally expected them to have "horns, a tail and eyes which glow in the dark, just as the radio programmes had described them". A Destexthe, *Rwanda: Essai sur le génocide* (Brussels: Editions Complexe, 1994), 50.

[20] ORINFOR is a parastatal organization which is responsible for all official media, the press, radio and television.

[21] As quoted by Radio France Internationale, 24 Jan. 1991. Reports on this incursion in the international media did not refer to any killing of civilians by the RPF.

[22] "Rwandan Radio alleges rebels attempt incursions via Gatuna and Ruhengeri", Radio Rwanda (French), 1800 GMT, 28 April 1991, *BBC Summary of World Broadcasts*, 1 May 1991. Mass killings of civilians were not reported to have been committed by the RPF before Feb. 1993.

Chapter 2

FROM EXTERNAL AGGRESSION TO THE ENEMY WITHIN: Incitement and State-Sponsored Violence (1990-1993)

Although President Habyarimana ordered citizens to assist in the battle against "infiltrators", he did not explicitly call for violence. However, in contrast to the vague rhetoric of high-level government officials, local civil servants directly instigated and organized several massacres of Tutsi civilians between 1990 and 1993.

1 Incitement to Violence by Administrative Officials: *"Massacres Téléguidés"*[1]

While clearly distinct from the fighting at the battle-front, the state-sponsored violence of 1990-1993 was incited and directed by Rwandan authorities who repeatedly invoked the war as a pretext to attack civilians. The first two such incidents occurred in north-west Rwanda, the general region affected by the war. These were the massacre in Kibilira *commune* in October 1990, and the killings of the Bagogwe[2] between January and February 1991.

Subsequent episodes, however, occurred far from the combat zones, such as the attacks in Murambi, eastern Rwanda (7-8 November 1991) when dozens of Tutsi were attacked and their homes pillaged; the killings of 85 Tutsi in Kibuye *préfecture* (August 1992); and the Bugesera massacre (March 1992). At first the attacks targeted only Tutsi civilians, however, by March 1992 they were also aimed at Hutu members of opposition parties. These killings were clearly organized by local government officials, specifically within their own administrative divisions, and generally did not spread to other areas.[3] From 1992 onwards, the militias affiliated with the MRND and the CDR, the *Interahamwe* and the *Impuzamugambi*, also played a role in executing the violence.

UN Special Rapporteur on Extrajudicial, Summary or Arbitrary Executions, Bacre Waly Ndiaye, writes that the role of administrative authorities in the violence "consists chiefly in encouraging, planning and directing the operation, and in some cases actually participating in it".[4] The authorities used false rumours and misinformation to promote ethnic hatred and incite the local residents to take part in the attacks on Tutsi civilians. Bacre Waly Ndiaye noted that a "study of the phases preceding outbreaks of violence among the population shows that such outbreaks are planned and prepared, with targets being identified in speeches by representatives of the authorities, broadcasts on Rwandan radio and leaflets".[5] Describing the methods used by local officials to instigate violence, Gérard Prunier claims the massacres were "preceded by political meetings during which a 'sensibilisation' process was carried out ... to put local peasants 'in the mood', to drum into them that the people they were to kill are *ibyitso* (accomplices), actual or potential collaborators of the RPF arch-enemy".[6]

The first attacks in Kibilira *commune*,[7] which occurred between 11 and 13 October 1990, 10 days after the start of the RPF offensive, and claimed the lives of 348 Tutsi civilians, illustrate this pattern of incitement and violence. According to testimony gathered by the International Commission of Investigation on Human Rights Violations in Rwanda Since October 1 1990, violence began in Kibilira following a meeting of Communal Councillors in which the *sous-préfet* produced two dead bodies and claimed that they were Hutu who had been murdered by Tutsi.[8] The *sous-préfet* ordered the Councillors to "'sensitize the population' to the importance of security measures" in their respective administrative divisions.[9] The same day, the *responsable de cellule* for Makoma, Gatumba *secteur*, is reported to have ordered people to set fire to the houses of Tutsi in that region, claiming that the *Inyenzi* planned to exterminate all the Hutu. Other administrative authorities in Gatumba sector instilled panic by spreading false rumours that a prominent regional authority, Colonel Serubuga, had been murdered. In the sectors of Kirengo, Ntobwe, Ngurugunzu and Karehe, administrative authorities falsely alleged that another major military figure, Colonel Uwihoreye, had been killed.

Although high-level government officials, including the then *préfet* of Gisenyi, Côme Bizimungu, and the Director of ORINFOR, Christophe Mfizi, as well as foreign diplomats, were aware of the violence, police failed to respond before 13 October. Following the killings, authorities blamed the incidents on both the RPF and Tutsi civilians. The Rwandan Embassy in Washington claimed on 11 October that RPF rebels were responsible for the killings and had used peasants as a shield during an attack. The next day, the Rwandan government alleged that the several hundred people massacred were rebels, killed in combat. On 13 October the government reported that the initial confusion arose because the rebels killed had all been disguised as civilians.[10] A report from the Office of the Public Prosecutor in Gisenyi later stated that the massacre had been incited by "Tutsi extremists", who encouraged the population to commit atrocities.

More state-sponsored violence occurred shortly after, probably in retaliation for the RPF raid on Ruhengeri town in late January 1991 (see Chapter 1, Section 2). These massacres, which were organized in several parts of the north-western *préféctures* of Ruhengeri and Gisenyi, killed between 300 and 1,000 Bagogwe.[11] According to the International Commission of Investigation the violence was systematically incited by local administrators, sometimes in collaboration with high-level authorities. In the *communes* of Gaseke and Giciye, the attacks began soon after the Minister of the Interior, Jean-Marie Vianney Mugemana, and the *préfet* of Ruhengeri, Charles Nzabageragaza, visited the region and issued a leaflet which stated: "Go do a special '*umuganda*'. Destroy all the bushes and all the [RPF] *Inkotanyi* [indomitable fighters] who are hiding there. And don't forget that those who are destroying weeds must also get rid of the roots".[12] "*Umuganda*" is the term for communal labour, usually agricultural or construction work, which was required of all Rwandans, over the age of 18, one day a week, from the 1970s.[13] This metaphor of killing as work had already been used in Mukingo *commune* on 12 October 1990, when the *bourgemestre,* Juvénal Kajerijeri, required residents to participate in a communal work project which involved the killing of two Bagogwe women. Communal labour also served as the pretext for civil servants in Giciye *commune* to assemble a large crowd on 2 February 1991 and order them to attack Bagogwe in that area.

In Mukingo and Kinigi *communes*, civil servants continued to direct violence against members of the Bagogwe population from late January to early February 1991. In Kinigi, between 30 and 60 Bagogwe were killed on 27 January after *bourgemestre* Thaddée Gasana ordered several communal councillors to round up and attack them with machetes and sticks.[14] In the Mukingo *commune, bourgemestre* Kajerijeri ordered local police to arrest the Bagogwe in the area, who were then killed by a group comprising local administrators, several teachers, and other citizens, using stones, spears and guns.

In other areas, the authorities invented reasons to justify their persecution of the Bagogwe. In Mutura *commune*, the Rwandan military — repeating the charade of 4-5 October 1990 in Kigali — enacted a fake RPF attack on the military camp at Bigogwe. The following day this attack was used as a pretext for soldiers and local administrative authorities to comb the area for RPA forces or "accomplices" who could have participated in the attack.[15]

The massacres of the Bagogwe occurred mostly in remote areas which were not easily accessible from the rest of the country, and information did not emerge about the bloodshed for several months. In August 1991, the RPF issued a communiqué calling for an international investigation into the violence but, although the RPF report was covered by both the national and international media, the Rwandan authorities denied that any violence had taken place. Instead, the government again invoked the war to explain away the disappearance of hundreds of Tutsi civilians, and maintained that massive numbers of Bagogwe had suddenly left the country to join the RPF.

2   The Bugesera Massacre and the Role of the Media

The Bugesera massacre of March 1992 was exacerbated by the print and broadcast media, which were used by the authorities as additional means of encouraging violence. The pogroms in this region were preceded by a series of attacks against Tutsi residents by administrative officials.[16] In October 1991, Fidèle Rwambuka, *Bourgemestre* of Kanzenze, ordered the arrest of several young Tutsi residents and accused them of preparing to join the RPF; 28 were briefly detained and eight disappeared. In mid-February 1992, five more civilians were arrested in connection with mine explosions which had occurred in the region, and were tortured.[17] In early March, a leaflet was distributed, allegedly by the authorities, following a verbal confrontation between members of the PL opposition and *Bourgemestre* Rwambuka. This accused PL supporters of working for the rebels, and stated: "They must not escape".[18]

In late November 1991, Hassan Ngeze, editor of the newspaper *Kangura* (notorious for its hate speech against Tutsi, and its connections with government officials – see Chapter 4) travelled to Bugesera and distributed anti-Tutsi leaflets throughout the region.[19] In addition, Bugesera was the subject of several false and inflammatory broadcasts by Radio Rwanda, including some reports which claimed that many young people from Bugesera had left the country to enlist in the RPF. Meanwhile, Jean-Baptiste Nubahumpatse, Radio Rwanda journalist and stringer for the BBC (British Broadcasting Corporation) French for Africa Service, filed a series of reports on mine explosions in Bugesera, falsely stating that a mine had been placed in front of the Kanzenze *bourgemestre*'s house and making unsubstantiated allegations that the RPF was responsible.[20]

On 3 March 1992, Radio Rwanda broadcast a communiqué from a fictitious organization, the *Commission inter-africaine de la non-violence*, said to be based in Nairobi. This communiqué, which was broadcast five times, warned that the fighting would soon move from traditional and guerrilla warfare to a "third phase" of the war which would consist of "assassinations" and "destruction of property".[21] According to the communiqué, this campaign of terror was to be carried out by "foreign terrorists", Africans and Arabs, who would infiltrate Rwanda under various guises, possibly as businessmen or tourists. Once in Rwanda, they would contact the alleged local head of the RPF, PL leader Justin Mugenzi — who in fact had no connection with the RPF — and initiate their plan to destroy Rwanda, starting with the assassination of 22 major political figures and businessmen. After the destruction had taken place, the communiqué predicted, RPF media organs would blame the violence on a political party dominated by Hutu.

This warning was followed the next day by an inflammatory communiqué from ORINFOR Director, Ferdinand Nahimana, which urged listeners to beware of the dangers at hand and to take preventative action. It urged listeners "to annihilate these machiavellian plans of the enemy *Inyenzi-Inkotanyi*".[22] Nahimana also added to the list of horrors predicted by the imaginary group in Nairobi: the "destabilization" process would include a campaign to provoke wide-spread civil disobedience and to demoralize the armed forces, driving them to resign or "lose their heads". He also claimed that the Nairobi group encompassed an equally fictitious organization based in Rwanda, the *Comité des sympathisants de non-violence au Rwanda*, which had begun to take steps to prevent the threatened violence.

In early March, members of the *Interahamwe* militia and the Presidential Guard, in civilian dress, were brought to the Bugesera region. During the night of 4-5 March, following Nahimana's broadcast, violence swept Kanzenze *commune*, killing mostly Tutsi. Within five days, 195 Tutsi and opposition supporters were massacred and subsequently the figure rose to 277,[23] with 15,000 persons displaced by the attacks. On 9 March, the Minister of the Interior denied international press reports that Tutsi were targeted in the massacres, and maintained that only 35 people had been killed. The next day Radio Rwanda reported that the cause of the violence was unclear but claimed: "some people are pointing the finger at the PL meeting held in Kanzenze on 1 March, which flogged [*sic*] local authorities and wounded the feelings of the population".[24] Prime Minister Sylvestre Nsanzimana publicly criticized ORINFOR for the incident, but no disciplinary action was taken against anyone involved. He merely issued a general warning to journalists and political party activists not to use inflammatory language.

The independent press in Rwanda and national human rights groups strongly condemned the government-sponsored violence and the role of the national radio in encouraging it. Five human rights associations issued a joint communiqué on 10 March 1992 which stated that the massacre was "a logical and direct response to the mysterious [Nahimana] communiqué which had been broadcast several times".[25] Largely as a result of these protests, Ferdinand Nahimana was dismissed from his position by the multi-party transitional government a few weeks after it was formed in April 1992.

3 Defining the Enemy: The Military Responds

The communiqués of March 1992 were not the first attempt to scare Rwandans with unlikely allegations about the dangers of enemies lurking amongst them. In December 1991, Radio Rwanda broadcast a communiqué from the military high command which accused the RPF of massively infiltrating different segments of civil society, including the private press and political parties, with the aim of sponsoring violence.[26]

During this period, the military formed a Commission of ten officers, led by Déogratias Nsabimana, to prepare a plan to conquer the enemy "on the battlefield, in politics and in the media".[27] On 21 September 1992, this group released a widely disseminated report which defined the main enemy as "Tutsi inside or outside the country, who are extremists and nostalgic for power, who have never recognized ... the realities of the Social Revolution of 1959, and who want to take power in Rwanda by any means, including by force". The document claimed that the enemies of Rwanda engaged in combat, espionage, and rumour-mongering, and even identified possible suspects, citing a list of newspapers and cultural associations it alleged were of a dubious nature. The report denounced "activists [who] ... turn public attention from the ethnic problem to the socio-economic divisions between rich and poor". The Commission listed people working in non-governmental organizations who, supposedly, were using their positions as fronts for the RPF. The text concluded that it was necessary for the public to be aware "to what extent the political and administrative authorities have been devoured" by the enemy.[28]

4 The Léon Mugesera Speech: Punishment for the Enemy

A speech given two months later by Léon Mugesera, Vice-President of the MRND in Gisenyi *préfecture*, represented the most explicit call for violence against Tutsi civilians and Hutu opposition supporters at that time. At a MRND rally in the *sous-préfecture* of Kabaya on 22 November 1992, Mugesera warned his audience to remain vigilant at all times. If provoked, they should forget the biblical notion of turning the other cheek and instead should meet violence with greater violence. Léon Mugesera claimed that the lessons of the Bible had changed: "I tell you that the Gospel has already changed in our movement. If someone gives you a slap, give him two in return, two fatal ones".[29]

Earlier in his speech, Mugesera had attacked the opposition parties in the transitional government of April 1992, led by Prime Minister Dismas Nsengiyaremye, from the MDR. He stated that MDR members should not be allowed to enter Gisenyi *préfecture* and exclaimed: "No infiltration in our stronghold: it is forbidden!" According to Mugesera, the Brussels meetings in mid-1992, between several opposition party representatives and RPF leaders, to initiate cease-fire negotiations, clearly showed that the opposition was working for the RPF. He castigated Prime Minister Nsengiyaremye for announcing that the government would consider plans to demobilize a number of army troops in order to create an army with 40 per cent RPA troops. Mugesera insisted that the Prime Minister, along with any other people who interfered with the defence of the nation, needed to be punished with "nothing less than death".

His speech also targeted Tutsi, referring to them as *Inyenzi*, and claimed that they had also threatened the security of the nation, not by representing the political interests of the RPF but rather by directly joining its ranks. He alleged that families throughout the southern *préfecture*s of Gikongoro and Butare were sending their children to join the RPF. Arguing that this was another crime, punishable by death, Mugesera demanded: "Why don't we arrest these people to exterminate them? Why don't we exterminate these people who send young people to the front?" He taunted his audience: "Tell me, are you really just waiting blissfully to be massacred?"

Should the justice system fail to carry out the punishment, Mugesera explained, people needed to take the law into their own hands, as justice should be executed "in the name of the people". Invoking religious authority, Mugesera also incited genocide against Tutsi: "we ourselves will take care of massacring these gangs of thugs. You know, it says in the Gospel that the snake comes to bite you and, if you let it stay, you are the one who will perish". He concluded: "the mistake we made in 1959 ... is that we let you get out safe and sound ... your country is Ethiopia and, soon, we will send you to your home, via Nyabarongo [river in Rwanda], on an express trip". During the genocide of 1994, Mugesera's statements were frequently repeated by Radio-Télévision Libre des Mille Collines (RTLM).[30]

Notes

[1] This expression is from Filip Reyntjens and means "massacres orchestrated and controlled from above".

[2] The Bagogwe are a Tutsi sub-group, mainly herdsmen, who have lived outside Tutsi traditional political structures since the seventeenth century. Fédération des droits de l'homme, Africa Watch, Union interafricaine des droits de l'homme et des peuples, Centre internationale des droits de la personne et du développement démocratique, *Report of the International Commission on Human Rights Violations in Rwanda Since October 1, 1990* (New York: Human Rights Watch/Africa, March 1993), 17.

[3] UN Economic and Social Council, *Extrajudicial, Summary or Arbitrary Executions, Addendum — Report by Mr B W Ndiaye, Special Rapporteur, on his mission to Rwanda from 8 to 17 April 1993*, UN Doc. E/CN.4/1994/7/Add.1., dated 11 Aug. 1993, 13. Later incidents in the north-west include: the attacks against Tutsi civilians in Kibilira *commune* in March 1992 and then again in Dec. 1992-Jan. 1993. On 26 Jan. 1993, just after the departure of the International Commission of Investigation, militia members, sometimes in junction with soldiers or local residents, killed 300 people in north-west Rwanda.

[4] Ibid., at 12.

[5] Ibid.

[6] G Prunier, *The Rwanda Crisis 1959-1994: History of a Genocide* (London and New York: Hurst & Company and Columbia University Press, 1995), 137-138.

[7] Kibilira *commune* is situated between Kigali and the capital of Gisenyi *préfecture*.

[8] The International Commission of Investigation on Human Rights Violations in Rwanda Since October 1, 1990 was comprised of representatives of four international human rights groups who visited Rwanda in January 1993 to investigate the state-sponsored violence and other human rights abuses which had occurred since the beginning of the war with the RPF. They had been

invited by several Rwandan human rights groups.

[9] Fédération internationale des droits de l'homme, Africa Watch, Union interafricaine des droits de l'homme et des peuples, and the Centre international des droits de la personne et du développement démocratique, *Report of the International Commission of Investigation on Human Rights Violations in Rwanda since October 1, 1990 (January 7-21, 1993) Final Report* (New York: Human Rights Watch/Africa, March 1993), 12.

[10] "Massacre Alleged", *Washington Post*, 11 Oct. 1990; "Rwanda Says Its Army Did Not Kill Civilians", *New York Times*, 12 Oct. 1990; and "Civilian Attack Denied", *Newsday*, 13 Oct. 1990.

[11] The exact figure has never been established; the victims were buried in unidentified graves. Prunier, note 6 above, at 137.

[12] Ibid., at 21.

[13] It was later abolished by the second transitional government appointed in April 1992.

[14] *Report of the International Commission*, note 9 above, at 19.

[15] Ibid., at 22.

[16] At that time, Bugesera comprised a large Tutsi population. It was relatively underpopulated until the 1960s when large numbers of displaced Tutsi moved there after being driven from other parts of the country during the Social Revolution of 1959-1961. The region includes the three communes of Kanzenze, Gashora and Ngenda. *Report of the International Commission*, note 9 above, at 25.

[17] *Report of the International Commission*, note 9 above, at 26.

[18] "Il ne faut pas qu'ils nous échappent". F Reyntjens, "Akazu, 'Escadrons de la mort' et autres 'Réseau Zéro': une historique des résistances au changement politique depuis 1990", in A Guichaoua (ed.), *Les crises politiques au Burundi et au Rwanda (1993-1994)*, (Lille/Paris: Université des Sciences et Technologies de Lille/Éditions Karthala, 1995), 268.

[19] Ibid., at 267. He cites a telegram from the Gako army camp addressed to the *Etat-Major*, which states that Hassan Ngeze travelled to the region "pour provoquer conflits interethniques".

[20] The reports claimed that a mine had been placed on the path leading to the house of the official when in fact it exploded about 5 km from there.

[21] Guichaoua, note 18 above, at 611-615.

[22] "De tels plans étant découverts, nous ne pouvons en tant que presse publique demeurer dans l'inaction. ... pour annihiler ces plans machiavéliques de l'ennemi *Inyenzi-Inkotanyi*". ("Communiqué de Ferdinand Nahimana, directeur de l'ORINFOR Office Rwandais d'Information", Kigali-Rwanda, 4 March 1992), as quoted in ibid., at 611-615.

[23] *Report of the International Commission*, note 9 above, at 27.

[24] Radio Rwanda, "Rwanda State of Siege declared in South after ethnic clashes" 10 March 1992 and "Rwandan Minister says situation normalising", *BBC Summary of World Broadcasts*, 11 March 1992.

[25] "La réplique logique et consécutive au mystérieux communiqué radiodiffusé à plusieurs reprises". "Déclaration des associations de défense des droits de l'homme sur les massacres de la population de la région Bugesera (Kigali, 10 March 1992)", Guichaoua, note 18 above, at 611-615.

[26] *Report of the International Commission* note 9 above, at 34.

[27] As quoted in ibid., at 35.

[28] Ibid.

[29] "Je vous dit que L'Évangile a déjà changé dans notre mouvement. Si on vous donne une gifle, donnez-en deux en retour, deux mortelles". "Discours de Léon Mugesera du 22 novembre 1992", in Guichaoua, note 18 above, at 620.

[30] In 1992 and later, during the 1994 genocide, Tutsi were dumped in the Nyabarongo River after being slaughtered.

On 12 July 1996, the Canadian government announced plans to expel Léon Mugesera from Canada, where he had lived since mid-1993, because of evidence that he had incited crimes against humanity in this speech. He lost the case brought against him in the Canadian court.

Chapter 3

SUPPRESSION OF INFORMATION

Incitement to violence, particularly by government officials, is all the more alarming when free speech and the right to information are restricted. In the absence of a diverse and truly independent media, propaganda becomes increasingly powerful. In Rwanda, a country which faced the fear and uncertainty of war, government officials easily manipulated information about the RPF and security issues as a pretext to incite violence against Tutsi civilians. Wartime measures, introduced to improve security, further exacerbated the lack of accurate information about the conflict by severely limiting the movement of people within the country.

In Rwanda, stringent limitations on the right to freedom of movement were introduced under the State of Emergency declared in November 1990, and applied retroactively to 1 October 1990, to prevent the RPA infiltrating the country. People were required to obtain a travel document from the administrative authorities, valid for only 30 days, just to leave their *commune*. Barriers, erected on major roads and at the entrances to towns, enforced these regulations. A night-time curfew was introduced throughout the country.[1] These measures were not evenly applied, as members of the ruling party, the MRND, received permanent *laissez-passers* enabling them to travel freely throughout the country, even at night.[2]

Wartime restrictions were relaxed by the transitional coalition government of April 1992 after the cease-fire which became effective from June 1992, but were reintroduced when the RPF resumed fighting in February 1993. They were relaxed once more several months later, except in the former front-line region. Even after these regulations were lifted, general residential requirements under Rwandan law (*1964 Loi postant résidence, recensement et cartes d'identité des Rwandais*) enabled the authorities to maintain close control over the population. This stipulated that all Rwandans were legally required to hold residence permits, in addition to national identity cards indicating their ethnicity. Landlords were responsible, under penalty of fines and imprisonment, for ensuring that all tenants had their papers in order. Under President Habyarimana's government, police checks, particularly in cities, were often used to ensure that all residents were properly registered. During the course of these inspections, people without valid documentation were sometimes deported to their areas of origin.[3]

The tight controls on the right to freedom of movement made it easier, in many cases, for authorities to cover up human rights abuses and to further promote their version of events, both about the war and the state-sponsored violence. The latter was generally described by officials as either a direct result or a by-product of the war,[4] if not attributable to the RPF itself. In some cases, survivors of massacres were prevented by the authorities from leaving their areas, for example, after the first Kibilira massacre in October 1990 and after the killings of the Bagogwe between January and February 1991. Restrictions on the movement of the Bagogwe appear to have been an important factor in suppressing news of their massacre for six months. Human Rights Watch reported that, in 1992, many people in Rwanda still did not believe that these massacres had occurred.

In other cases, the authorities used more specific means to isolate areas where atrocities were in process. Telephone lines were suddenly cut during the Bugesera massacre of March 1992 and also in the *préfectures* of Gisenyi, Ruhengeri and Kibuye during the killings of January 1993. An official inquiry into the January 1993 killings found that the communications system resumed service, without requiring repairs, after the killing had finished.[5]

In rural or remote areas, this absence of information about human rights violations as they occur is clearly a factor which facilitates their being committed in the first place. During his mission of April 1993, UN Special Rapporteur Bacre Waly Ndiaye noted that episodes of state-sponsored violence in Rwanda often ceased only after the killings were reported by journalists and human rights groups. To redress this situation, he recommended that a system be introduced "for sending information rapidly from the place where the violence is occurring directly to a security service responsible for taking action, for example, via radio link".[6]

1   Ruling the Airwaves

With a high illiteracy rate and many people living in rural areas, where movement is greatly restricted, tight government control of the airwaves enabled the Rwandan authorities to suppress crucial information about the war and the killings of Tutsi civilians.[7] Radio is the most important means of mass communication throughout all of sub-Saharan Africa, and most countries still do not have an independent broadcasting service or fair and accountable licensing procedures for private radio stations.[8] Rwanda has been no exception. Although Article 16 of the Press Law (no. 54/91) of 15 Nov. 1991 stipulates that "the freedom to establish and operate a radio or television station is guaranteed to every person", during the Second Republic the licensing procedure was regulated by government bodies and this practice has continued under the RPF. Applicants were required to submit their proposals to the Ministry of Information. The applications were then passed to a government commission for consideration and recommendation. This commission was composed of one representative each from the Ministries of Information, the Interior, Justice, Defence, and a representative from the Prime Minister's office. The final decision on the application was made by the Cabinet.

In Rwanda, however, the manipulation of information by the government has been facilitated by the fact that, whilst few Rwandans outside of major cities speak French or English, the entire population speaks Kinyarwanda. Most people are dependent on Radio Rwanda for news and general information, particularly given that no foreign radio stations have broadcast in Kinyarwanda until very recently.[9] In April 1992, opposition representatives in the newly-formed coalition government began a difficult struggle to retrieve Radio Rwanda from the firm grip of the MRND.

By mid-1992, Rwandans in all but the south were able to tune into Radio Muhabura, the RPF radio station, broadcasting from Uganda, and named after a mountain in northern Rwanda which means "leading the way". Although this station broke the government monopoly on broadcasting, it did little to contribute to the free flow of information. Instead, as its name suggests, Radio Muhabura continued the culture of propaganda and counter-propaganda, providing little concrete information about events and spending a lot of air time presenting and promoting the RPF to the Rwandan population.

ORINFOR: the struggle for reform

Shortly after taking power in the 1973 *coup d'état*, President Habyarimana abolished the Ministry of Information and replaced it with the Rwandan Office of Information, ORINFOR, which controlled all government media and was, until 1991, directly responsible to the President's office.[10] The *9 Octobre 1974 Décret-loi sur la création de l'Office Rwandais d'Information*, established ORINFOR as a parastatal organization whose activities were overseen by a seven-member Board of Directors which defined "the direction of the establishment's activities in accordance with the country's political orientation (Article 4)".[11] In addition, the Board of Directors was responsible for all matters relating to ORINFOR's budget. Under the 1974 law, ORINFOR's Director and Board of Directors were appointed by the President (Articles 4 and 19). The Director of ORINFOR, who also served as the official spokesperson of the President's office, was responsible for supervising the activities of the department and its personnel, who were nominated by the Board of Directors and appointed by Presidential Decree (Article 21).

The Ministry of Information was formally reintroduced in December 1991 with the establishment of the transitional government led by Prime Minister Sylvestre Nsanzimana. In response to growing concern at the lack of an independent public broadcasting system, the trusteeship of ORINFOR was removed from the President's office and assumed by the Ministry of Information. In practice, however, ORINFOR has always remained close to the President's office and operates independently of the Ministry of Information. Even under the RPF, ORINFOR continues to exercise almost complete control over the government media, from Radio Rwanda to the national television and government newspapers.

On 22 December 1990, almost two months after the RPF invasion, Christophe Mfizi, the Director of ORINFOR, who had held the position since 1974, was dismissed and replaced by Ferdinand Nahimana. According to former colleagues, Christophe Mfizi had tried to practise a policy of relative openness at ORINFOR, despite constant pressure from the President's office and other high-level officials. In contrast, Nahimana was already notorious for his extreme political views and prejudice against Tutsi, having participated along with figures such as Léon Mugesera, in the 1973 *Comité de Salut Public*, the movement which tried to exclude Tutsi from the universities. Nahimana had no journalistic experience, but had previously been employed as a Professor of History at the Ruhengeri campus of the University of Rwanda.

Although the appointment of Nahimana as ORINFOR's Director reinforced the domination of the MRND on national radio, with the legalization of opposition political parties in mid-1991, this exclusion was soon challenged. Radio Rwanda came under mounting pressure to serve as a forum in which opposition political parties could present their views. On 17 November 1991, the MDR, PL, and PSD held a rally of 20,000 people in Kigali to press for equal access to Radio Rwanda, along with other demands, such as an end to the harassment of opposition supporters. A few days later Radio Rwanda announced that representatives of several political parties had met with Nahimana and had succeeded in obtaining 15 minutes of airtime weekly for each major opposition party.[12] This move proved limited in that it did not otherwise affect the content of radio programmes. It did, however, allow the political parties some access to a vital forum for communication, and seems to have been an important factor in facilitating the rise in support for opposition parties over the next several months.

In April 1992, when the second transitional government came to power, opposition party members in the cabinet successfully pressed for Nahimana's dismissal. Although, officially, he was removed for censoring the speeches of the incoming Prime Minister and MDR member, Dismas Nsengiyaremye, it is widely acknowledged that Nahimana was forced to leave office because of the inflammatory communiqués which were broadcast prior to the Bugesera massacre. He was then appointed as a diplomat and sent to Germany, but returned to his teaching position when the German government refused him diplomatic recognition.

The position of ORINFOR's Director was vacant for over a year as the President and the MRND cabinet members succeeded in blocking all candidates put forward by the opposition. Following the

47

appointment in April 1992 of PSD member Pascal Ndengejeho as Minister of Information, opposition parties enjoyed slightly better access to the national radio station which began to provide some coverage of their activities. The impact of the Minister of Information was limited, however, as key posts within ORINFOR continued to be occupied by hardline MRND members during the 15-month interim period before a permanent Director was appointed. Efforts by Pascal Ndengejeho to introduce structural reform within ORINFOR and the Ministry of Information were thwarted by the government.

Overall, the reporting remained heavily biased in favour of the MRND as Prospère Musemakweli, ORINFOR's interim Director, allowed several journalists close to President Habyarimana to maintain control of the most important news programmes at Radio Rwanda.[13] Musemakweli, the former Head of Administration and Finance, was not a journalist and, as a result, reportedly gave the department heads complete autonomy, making no effort to check their pro-MRND bias. Meanwhile, the president of the Board of Directors, Spérancie Karwera Mutwe, was a staunch MRND supporter and the Board itself was largely dominated by MRND members. With these internal pressures, ORINFOR continued to broadcast blatantly false reports of alleged abuses by the RPF. After the RPF resumed the war on 8 February 1993, Radio Rwanda provided a grossly exaggerated report that the RPF had killed 500 persons at the Rebero camp for the internally displaced.[14] On 20 February, the Minister of Information wrote a letter to the Director of the radio station, asking him to account for the erroneous report.[15]

Meanwhile, information about human rights abuses in Rwanda was still often suppressed by the national radio station. In 1992 and 1993, Rwandan human rights groups reported that they were sometimes denied the opportunity to issue communiqués on the radio. And, in April 1993, UN Special Rapporteur Bacre Waly Ndiaye noted that Radio Rwanda's "two different language versions of reports of the press conference he had given in order to put an end to rumours concerning the objectives of his mission contradicted each other".[16]

Following the July 1993 appointment of a third transitional government, led by Prime Minister Agathe Uwilingiyimana, President Habyarimana and the MRND cabinet members finally agreed to accept MDR member Jean-Marie Vianney Higiro as Director of

ORINFOR. A few months earlier he had won a national competition which was held to resolve the political deadlock over the post. This concession was part of an attempt by the President to build a closer alliance with the incoming Prime Minister, whom he had strongly supported over other proposed MDR candidates. Higiro took up the position on 8 August 1993, but was somewhat restricted in his attempts to improve the independence of reporting at Radio Rwanda by virtue of the fact that a large number of journalists at the station and ORINFOR board members were pro-MRND.

Although many observers noted that the quality of Radio Rwanda broadcasts generally improved, with less bias, under Higiro and the new Minister of Information, Faustin Rucogoza, incidents of incorrect and inflammatory reporting occasionally still occurred. One observer reported that, in December 1993, Radio Rwanda broadcast an interview with a woman in Byumba *préfecture* who stated that the RPF had massacred a group of people. She claimed to have been beaten with a hammer and then tossed, along with all the corpses, into a mass grave, 20 metres deep. The woman maintained that she had managed to climb from the pit, just in time to witness several RPF soldiers remove a foetus from a pregnant woman, and then immediately force her to prepare a meal for them. Although neither her ascent from the deep grave nor the cooking by the recently disembowelled woman were physically probable, this fantastic tale was presented by Radio Rwanda as a serious report.

Radio Muhabura: "leading the way"

In mid-1991, the creation of Radio Muhabura was reported by Radio Rwanda, Reuters and the Ugandan government daily newspaper, *The New Vision*. Radio Rwanda immediately instructed listeners not to believe anything which they heard on the rebel radio broadcasts and warned: "whenever you will hear anything from that radio station, try to understand their aim which is ... to divide our country and try to put back our country in to the thirties".[17]

The broadcasts were not detected by the BBC Monitoring Service in Nairobi until a year later, after which point they were received regularly. The BBC first monitored Radio Muhabura for one hour in the early evening of 2 July 1992 on 6400 FM kHz, when the radio began its broadcasts with the following announcement: "This is Radio Muhabura. Radio Muhabura, the voice that repatriates, the voice of the RPF *Inkotanyi*".[18] The programme followed with classical music and a discussion on the Rwandan Constitution. Radio Muhabura broadcast regularly from that time onwards, often pirating BBC radio broadcasts, and continued throughout the entire genocide of 1994.

Clearly it would have been difficult for any RPF journalist to enter Rwandan territory to conduct on-site investigations, and Radio Muhabura relied heavily on a series of confidential contacts for information on developments in Rwanda. Perhaps for this reason Radio Muhabura focused on the RPF rather than on events within Rwanda, which it was claiming to "liberate". Radio Muhabura broadcast official statements by RPF leaders, and generally tried to encourage people to support the movement in its battle against the Habyarimana government and the FAR. The station relayed the official RPF explanation of its decision to attack Rwanda, claiming that "arms were necessary" for Rwandans to "regain their rights". Radio Muhabura made sweeping allegations about the "extremist" Rwandan government, without reference to the political changes brought about by the transitional coalition of April 1992. It accused the government of systematically fomenting ethnic and regional divisions within the country and practising arbitrary arrests and imprisonment. By mid-1992, however, the coalition government had already achieved some progress in the legal protection of human rights, and incidents of arbitrary arrests began to decrease.

Although it should not have been difficult for Radio Muhabura to discredit MRND government officials, given the violence by the *Interahamwe* militia of the MRND, or the activities of the "Network Zero" death squad (see Political Background chapter), Radio Muhabura failed to do so convincingly because its reports were largely vague and unsubstantiated. On the issue of state-sponsored violence, Radio Muhabura often indicated that incidents had occurred but failed to provide much concrete evidence. Following the massacres in north-western Rwanda in January 1993, Radio Muhabura reported: "the Kigali regime has now embarked on genocide, destruction and looting of people's property. There is concrete evidence to [*sic*] this. Killings have systematically been perpetrated in *communes*. ... The Rwandan army and other security organs are merely looking on as these massacres are committed".[19] Although the station alleged that genocide was taking place, it did not state anything specific to support this claim and failed to explain that Tutsi were being systematically targeted in the violence.[20] Another broadcast, on 25 October 1992, made the ambiguous claim that armed militia of the MRND had "devised traps aimed at exterminating the youth". In the latter case, it remained unclear precisely what the radio was alleging.

Meanwhile, Radio Muhabura systematically denied all reports of abuses by RPA troops, even when there was substantial evidence to the contrary. After the RPF broke the cease-fire and invaded Rwanda on 8 February 1993, its soldiers summarily executed eight administrative officials and several of their relatives in Ruhengeri town. It was also reported that the RPF killed as many as 100 other civilians during this incursion.[21] Three days later, Radio Muhabura claimed that any allegation of killings by the RPF must necessarily be false. It stated: "To kill innocent citizens is a shameful crime that the RPF could not dare commit. ... Ever since taking up arms, the RPF has wanted to protect citizens who were being killed by the MRND".[22]

2   Restrictions on the Independent Press and Human Rights Reporting

In Rwanda, an independent press has existed alongside the official media since before Independence. *Kinyamateka*, a monthly newspaper in Kinyarwanda, affiliated with the Roman Catholic Church, was created in 1933 and greatly expanded in 1955, with circulation rising from 5,000 to 20,000, after Grégoire Kayibanda, future President of Rwanda, became its editor.[23] The newspaper then served as a vehicle for the ideas behind the Social Revolution, repeatedly arguing that the "Hutu majority" must have political representation. It was joined in 1967 by the bi-monthly *Dialogue*,[24] another independent Catholic publication. Both publications enjoyed protection from government harassment by virtue of their association with the Catholic Church, which was an extremely powerful institution from the colonial period onward. Nevertheless, in the post-Independence period, both newspapers generally had to refrain from directly criticizing the government or its treatment of Tutsi, who were systematically targeted for abuse and discrimination during both the First and Second Republics.[25]

In 1988, a truly independent press began to emerge, starting with the establishment of the Kinyarwandan publication *Kanguka* (Wake Up), by Valens Kajeguhakwa, a Tutsi businessman. It was followed, in early 1990, by several other newspapers, mostly in Kinyarwanda but with some articles in French: *Umuranga, Ijambo, Isibo, Le démocrate* and *Kangura*.[26] The latter was essentially a government-backed parody of *Kanguka*, founded by Hassan Ngeze, who used to work there (see Chapter 4).

Although the independent press had both pre-dated and advocated a transition to democracy, it quickly expanded with the advent of multi-party politics. Within a few months of the legalization of opposition parties in June 1991, the number of independent newspapers in Rwanda rose from about a dozen to 60, most of which were either affiliated with or financed by various opposition parties or by the ruling party, the MRND. Many of these newspapers had ceased publication after the first year, however, and by 1992, there were only 30 newspapers still publishing.[27]

The nascent press in Rwanda was confronted with many of the same pressures and restrictions prevalent in other countries which have not yet made a full transition to democracy. Journalists were subject to arbitrary arrest and detention; newspapers were seized and confiscated by the authorities. The Press Law (no. 54/91) of 15 November 1991 requires newspapers to deposit copies of all issues to the administrative and judicial authorities, and provides for severe penalties, including prison terms, for offences such as defamation of the Head of State.[28] Article 166 of the 1977 Penal Code introduced a vague definition of sedition which amounts to a sweeping restriction on free speech. It declares that it is a crime, punishable by 2-10 years in prison and by a fine of Rwfr2,000 to Rwfr200,000 (US$12 and US$1,189 respectively – in 1993 168.2 Rwandan francs = US$1), to

> incite the population to revolt against the established authorities, either to incite or attempt to incite conflict amongst the population or to cause

52

alarm and seek to bring turmoil to the territory of
the Republic.[29]

In addition to this general harassment, the war brought further
restrictions. The limitations on freedom of movement hampered
independent journalists in their ability to conduct on-site investigations away from their areas of residence, particularly in the north, where
it was dangerous to travel. Newspaper distribution was disrupted by
the tight control on movement in between administrative divisions.[30]
Moreover, journalists who criticized the government, especially in
relation to its handling of the RPF invasion, risked denunciation by
the authorities as " the enemy", "RPF supporters" or "accomplices".
They could also be targeted by Article 47 of the 1991 Press Law, which
states that it is a crime, punishable by 2-10 years in prison and by a
fine of Rfwr50,000 to Rwfr500,000 (US$297 and US$2,973
respectively), to provoke Rwandan soldiers "in order to divert them
from their military duties or from their obedience to their superiors".[31]

Between 1990 and mid-1992, there were 41 cases of journalists
being harassed by the authorities, arbitrarily detained, or arrested and
brought to trial. Many of these incidents involved journalists accused
of working for the RPF. In July 1990, *Kanguka* journalist Vincent
Rwabukwisi was detained immediately after conducting an interview
in Nairobi with the former King of Rwanda, Kigeri Ndahindurwa
(Kigeri V). Several months later he was accused of participating in the
RPF invasion and finally charged with "threatening state security".
On 22 October he was sentenced to 15 years' imprisonment, although
he was later released in May 1991 (see Chapter 4).

In other cases, the interests of national security were used to
suppress the reporting of state-sponsored violence against civilians.
Government officials issued several warnings to independent journalists telling them not to step out of line and, in May 1991, the Council
of Ministers announced that elements of the private press were
threatening national security. Radio Rwanda reported:

> The government recalled that freedom of
> expression should be carried out within the limits
> set by the laws and regulations in force in our
> country. The exercise of this freedom should not

be synonymous with disinformation, intoxification [*sic*] and, more importantly, not be an attack on the morale of our armed forces. The national press is therefore called upon to stop publishing subversive items which, by their nature, weaken the national cohesion which is needed more today than ever before in order to win the war. ...[32]

According to this report, any criticism of government policies would constitute "disinformation", and negative coverage of the Rwandan troops, including articles on their losses to the RPF, would be classified as "an attack on the morale of our armed forces"; nothing less than treason. Less than two weeks later, journalists François-Xavier Hangimana, of the weekly *Ijambo*, and Charles Karinganire, Adrien Rangira and Vincent Rwabukwisi, of *Kanguka*, were arrested and charged under Articles 166 and 391 of the Penal Code.[33] Enoch Ruhigira, government spokesperson and *Ministre d'Etat* (Adviser to the President) claimed the four were guilty of "consciously or unconsciously playing the enemy's game".[34] They were detained for several months and then released.

Similarly, the December 1991 communiqué by the FAR, broadcast on Radio Rwanda, which claimed that sections of the independent media were working for the RPF, also served to intimidate independent journalists (see Chapter 2, section 3). Immediately after the broadcast, seven journalists went into hiding for several weeks.[35] Two of these, Théotime Kamanayo and Godefroid Nshimiyimana, were arbitrarily detained less than a week after the broadcast.

On 3 December, Boniface Ntawuyirushintege, Editor of *Umurangi*, was arrested at his home and beaten by members of the *Service central des renseignements* (Central Intelligence Service – SCR). On 10 December, *Kanguka* journalists Obed Bazimaziki and Adrien Rangira were held at a national printing company, *l'Imprimerie nationale*, by the SCR. Antoine Mbarushimana, Publication Director of *Le Soleil*, was separately detained briefly at the same location. The reasons for these detentions were unknown.[36]

On 29 March 1992, human rights activist Fidèle Kanyabugoyi, a Bagogwe and also a representative of the organization Kanyarwanda, was arrested. This group had just published a letter protesting the killings of Tutsi in the Bugesera region and, at the time of his arrest, Kanyabugoyi had been in the process of documenting the 1991 attacks on the Bagogwe. The authorities confiscated all his records on human rights abuses and charged him with jeopardizing the security of the State. In April, he obtained provisional release but was not allowed to travel freely thereafter.[37] He was later beaten to death by the *Interahamwe* on 12 April 1994.

From formal to informal repression

Following the introduction of the multi-party transitional government in April 1992, journalists and human rights activists enjoyed greater legal protection from the authorities and there were far fewer cases of arbitrary arrest and detention. From April 1992 until the end of 1993, there were only three reported cases of interference with journalistic activities by government authorities.[38] The authorities also took steps to improve the legal framework for the press. Minister of Information Faustin Rucogoza initiated a draft law to abolish all import tax on paper and ink.[39] In addition, in 1993, he was responsible for developing a revised draft Press Law in consultation with legal experts, human rights activists and several journalists associations.[40]

Just as formal respect for freedom of expression was improving, government critics were increasingly subject to informal repression with the emergence in 1992 of militias affiliated to the MRND and the extremist CDR. In addition to orchestrating state-sponsored violence, these militias played a major role from 1992 onwards in attacking and intimidating government critics, particularly journalists and human rights activists. Another clandestine organization, "Network Zero", similarly targeted outspoken critics.

The existence of "Network Zero" was first disclosed by Christophe Mfizi, former Director of ORINFOR, who coined the expression, and was then established more definitively in October 1992 by Professor Filip Reyntjens.[41] UN Special Rapporteur Bacre Waly Ndiaye, reporting on his April 1993 mission to Rwanda, said that although he could not prove that the militias or the death squad had been behind particular attacks on individuals, he had little doubt about the strength of these clandestine organizations. He stated that there were "sufficient indications to enable the Special Rapporteur to conclude that a second power exists alongside that of the official authorities".[42]

This "second power" soon came to represent the biggest threat to independent journalists and human rights activists in Rwanda. The death squad and militia groups used death threats, physical attacks and political assassinations to terrorize and intimidate government critics. In 1993, all cases of attacks on journalists in Rwanda reported by the Committee to Protect Journalists (CPJ) involved physical assaults or killings rather than arrests and imprisonment. For example, on 6 April 1993, television producer Callixte Kalisa was shot dead close to his home in Remera, Kigali. He had found a grenade near the entrance to his home several days before. In early May, Ignace Ruhatana, Editor of *Kanyarwanda*, published by the human rights group of the same name, was attacked by a group of unidentified people who attempted to steal his documents on human rights issues. Several months later, in mid-November 1993, the prominent human rights activist and then Public Prosecutor Alphonse-Marie Nkubito was the target of a grenade attack just outside his home. Though seriously injured, he survived the attack.

Although it was not often possible to prove precisely who was responsible for a given attack, in some instances militia leaders openly admitted that they were planning to harass or eliminate particular individuals. In late 1993, Ali Yusuf Mugenzi, a journalist at Radio Rwanda and BBC Swahili Service stringer, was targeted by the *Interahamwe* on account of a report he had filed with the BBC concerning a violent confrontation between MRND and MDR supporters in Kigali, which assessed the *Interahamwe's* intimidation of opposition members. The night of the planned attack, Mugenzi was tipped off by two contacts within the MRND, who informed him that his BBC report that day had upset party leaders. One of them, a colleague from Radio Rwanda, took Mugenzi to meet Sued Ndayitabi, the *Interahamwe* leader responsible for militia in Biryogo *secteur*, Kigali, in order to "apologize". The militia leader is reported to have admitted that earlier he had ordered several members to assault Mugenzi that very evening, but was persuaded by the MRND member present to cancel the plan.

Suppression of Information

Despite efforts by members of the transitional government and several Public Prosecutors to halt militia activity, the situation seriously deteriorated. Distribution of arms and ammunition to the militias had been reported as early as 1992 but accelerated dramatically in 1993 and early 1994. Also in late 1993, military training became more vigorous, as groups of approximately 300 militia members at a time were brought to a military camp in the north-east region of Mutara.[43] In early 1994, additional training of militias by the Presidential Guard was reported at the Kanombe barracks in Kigali, as well as in military camps in Gabiro, north-east Kigali and in Bigogwe, Gisenyi *prefécture*.[44] The militias became visibly more powerful during this period, to the extent that they threw up roadblocks in many areas of the capital and regularly harassed people trying to pass. After the CDR leader Martin Bucyana was lynched by a crowd in Butare *préfecture* on 23 February 1994, in response to the assassination of PSD leader Félicien Gatabazi a few days previously, militias retaliated by killing some 30 people in the neighbourhood of Gikondo, a CDR stronghold in Kigali. Dozens of Tutsi families living there were forced to move to other areas of the capital. In February 1994, *Rwanda Rushya* journalist Joseph Mudatsikira described the situation:

> Terror reigns in the city of Kigali and the surround-
> ing area. People have been killed, injured, and
> dispossessed of their goods; houses have been
> pillaged and destroyed. ... The authors of these
> excesses are known: the MRND and CDR militias,
> supported by the Presidential Guard and the
> gendarmes.[45]

The militias also became stronger outside the Kigali area. Human rights activist Joseph Matata, Executive Secretary of the *Association Rwandaise pour la Défense des Droits de l'Homme* (Rwandan human rights association — ARDHO), reported that in December 1993 repeated threats by militia leaders in his home *préfecture* of Kibungo compelled him to flee the area and live for several months at his office in downtown Kigali.

Notes

[1] See, US Department of State, *Country Reports on Human Rights Practices for 1991* (Washington: US Government Printing Office, 1992), 302-311.

[2] F Reyntjens, "Akazu, 'Escadrons de la mort' et autres 'Réseau Zéro': une historique des résistances au changement politique depuis 1990" in A Guichaoua (ed.), *Les crises politiques au Burundi et au Rwanda (1993-1994)*, (Lille/Paris: Université des Sciences et Technologies de Lille/Éditions Karthala, 1995), 266.

[3] See US Department of State, *Country Reports on Human Rights Practices for 1993* (Washington: US Government Printing Office, 1994), 226-235. The Special Rapporteur on Extrajudicial, Summary or Arbitrary Executions, Bacre Waly Ndiaye, noted the "striking contrast between, on the one hand, the close control exercised over the population and the detailed partitioning of the territory ... and, on the other, the absence of any structure for the protection of vulnerable populations, more particularly the Tutsi minority". UN Economic and Social Council, *Extrajudicial, Summary or Arbitrary Executions, Addendum — Report by Mr B W Ndiaye, Special Rapporteur, on his mission to Rwanda from 8 to 17 April 1993*, UN Doc. E/CN.4/1994/7/Add.1., dated 11 Aug. 1993, 14.

[4] A Human Rights Watch report notes that in a speech on 25 Jan. 1993, President Habyarimana claimed that the violence taking place in the northwest was "a popular reaction against the Arusha Accords and made no effort to condemn it". Later, in the correspondence to the Fédération internationale des droits de l'homme, Habyarimana claimed that the RPF invasion caused ethnic conflicts between the Hutu and Tutsi. Africa Watch, *Beyond the Rhetoric: Continuing Human Rights Abuses in Rwanda* (New York: Human Rights Watch, June 1993), 17.

[5] UN Economic and Social Council, note 3 above, at 16.

[6] Ibid., at 18.

[7] 44 per cent of the population is illiterate. Joint Evaluation of Emergency Assistance to Rwanda, *The International Response to Conflict and Genocide: Lessons from the Rwanda Experience (Study I: Historical Perspective: Some Explanatory Factors)*, (Denmark: Steering Committee of the Joint Evaluation of Emergency Assistance to Rwanda, March 1996), 17.

[8] On the issue of state control of broadcasting in sub-Saharan Africa, see: ARTICLE 19 and Index on Censorship, *Who Rules the Airwaves?*

Suppression of Information

Broadcasting in Africa (London: March 1995).

[9] After the 1994 genocide for example, the BBC introduced a Kinyarwanda programme to help reunite separated families, which includes a news bulletin.

[10] The internal structure of ORINFOR is defined by: *8 août 1978-Arrêté Présidentiel N.273/01, Organisation et attribution des services de l'Office Rwandais d'Information (J.O., 1978, 473).*

[11] "Les lignes générales de l'action de l'établissment en conformité avec l'orientation politique générale du pays". (*J.O., 1974,* 588).

[12] Radio Rwanda (French), "Rwandan political parties to have regular air-time," 24 Nov. 1991, *BBC Summary of World Broadcasts.*

[13] Three journalists who were later to become RTLM shareholders, all from the north, held key positions: Jean-Baptiste Bamwanga worked as the Editor-in-Chief of Radio News; Joseph Serugendo was retained as the Head of Technical Services at ORINFOR; and Froduald Ntawulkura served as Head of Radio Programmes, the department which produced thematic programmes, for example, on women and children.

[14] During this attack, the RPF executed eight civil servants and nine of their relatives in Ruhengeri town. Elsewhere, up to 100 other civilians were reported to have been killed. Africa Watch, *Beyond the Rhetoric: Continuing Human Rights Abuses in Rwanda*, Vol. 5., No. 7 (New York: Human Rights Watch, June 1993), 24-25.

[15] Ibid., at 16.

[16] UN Economic and Social Council, note 3 above, at 17.

[17] Radio Rwanda, Kigali (English), 1430 GMT, 13 June 1991, *BBC Summary of World Broadcasts.*

[18] BBC Summary of World Broadcasts, "Rwandan rebel radio heard", *The Monitoring Report*, 7 July 1992.

[19] Radio Muhabura (English), 0030 GMT, 30 Jan. 1993, "Kigali regime continues with massacres", *BBC Summary of World Broadcasts*, 2 Feb. 1993.

[20] Radio Muhabura almost never mentioned the terms "Hutu" or "Tutsi", possibly because the RPF leadership tried not to call attention to the Front's own ethnic composition.

[21] Africa Watch, note 14 above, at 24-25.

[22] Radio Muhabura (Kinyarwanda), 1715 GMT, 11 Feb. 1993, *BBC Summary*

of World Broadcasts, 13 Feb. 1993.

[23] *Kinyamateka* enjoyed a widespread distribution service through the Church, which was strongly established throughout the country.

[24] Since 1991, *Dialogue* has been a monthly publication.

[25] There were a few exceptions to this pattern. In 1968, *Kinyamateka* journalist Félicien Semusambi accused the government of practising corruption, nepotism and regional discrimination. He was imprisoned, and later fled the country, and Editor, Father Maida was expelled (Semusambi was later killed during the genocide). Later, in 1986, Director, Sylvio Sindambiwe tried to introduce more critical reporting but was soon subject to threats and physical attacks. He died in a mysterious car accident three years later. *Kinyamateka* became a truly independent newspaper under Father André Sibomana, who became Director in 1988.

[26] F Reyntjens, *L'Afrique des Grands Lacs en crise: Rwanda, Burundi: 1988-1994* (Paris: Éditions Karthala, 1994), 171.

[27] US Department of State, *Country Reports on Human Rights Practices for 1992* (Washington: US Government Printing Office, 1993), 206-214.

[28] *Loi n.54/91 du 15 novembre 1991 sur la presse (J.O. N.23 du 1er décembre 1991)*, 1866-1878.

[29] "Exciter les populations contre les pouvoirs établis, soit soulevé ou tenter de soulever les citoyens les uns contre les autres, soit alarmé les populations et cherché ainsi à porter les troubles sur le territoire de la République." *Code pénal Rwandais, Livre II, Décret-loi N. 21/77*, 18 August 1977, *(J.O.*, 1978, n.1, *Section II: Des atteintes à la sûreté de l'Etat)*.

[30] J-M Vianney Higiro, "Plaidoyer pour une politique nationale de l'information," *Dialogue*, no. 147 (Kigali), juillet-août 1991, 108.

[31] "Dans le but de les détourner de leurs devoirs militaires et de l'obéissance qu'ils doivent à leurs chefs".

[32] Radio Rwanda (French), 1100 GMT, Kigali, 15 May 1991, "Rwandan government tells press not to abuse freedom and undermine army morale", *BBC Summary of World Broadcasts*, 17 May 1991.

[33] Committee to Protect Journalists, *Attacks on the Press 1991* (New York: CPJ, 1991), 52-53. Charles Karinganire and Vincent Rwabukwisi were later killed in the 1994 genocide.

[34] As quoted in Reuters, "Rwanda detains journalists, delays legislation of opposition parties," 4 June 1991.

[35] They are André Kameya, Director of *Rwanda Rushya*; Jean-Pierre Mugabe, Director of *Le Tribun du Peuple*; Théoneste Muberantwali, of *Nyabarongo*; Edouard Mutsinzi, from *Le Messager*; Théotime Kamanayo, Vincent Shabakaka and Godefroid Nshimiyimana, of *Kiberinka*. André Kameya, Théotime Kamanayo and Vincent Shabakaka were later killed in the genocide.

[36] Committee to Protect Journalists, note 33 above, at 52.

[37] Amnesty International, *Amnesty International Report 1993* (London: 1993), 249.

[38] Committee to Protect Journalists, *Attacks on the Press* 1992 (New York: CPJ, 1993), 78.

[39] Faustin Rucogoza, "Allocution de Clôture", *Dialogue*, no. 175 (Brussels: April-May 1994), 112.

[40] Although never enacted, it proposed fines instead of prison sentences for a number of offences and required the state to offer financial and logistical support to the private press. (See Ministère de l'Information, *Rapport du seminaire de révision de la loi sur la presse*, 15-16 Dec. 1993)

[41] G Prunier, *The Rwanda Crisis 1959-1994: History of a Genocide* (London and New York: Hurst & Company and Columbia University Press, 1995), 168.

[42] UN Economic and Social Council, note 3 above, at 13.

[43] Human Rights Watch, *Genocide in Rwanda: April-May 1994*, Vol. 6, No. 4 (New York: Human Rights Watch, May 1994), 2.

[44] African Rights, *Death, Despair and Defiance*, Revised Edition (London: African Rights, 1995), 54.

[45] "La terreur règne dans la ville de Kigali et dans ses environs. Des personnes sont tuées, blessées et dépossédées; des maisons sont pillées et détruites. ... Les auteurs de ces exactions sont connus: les milices des partis MRND et CDR, appuyées par les gardes présidentiels et les gendarmes". Joseph Mudatsikira, *Rwanda Rushya*, no. 54, Feb. 1994, 5-6.

Chapter 4

THE RISE OF "HATE MEDIA" AND ITS GOVERNMENT SPONSORSHIP

1   Print Media: *Kangura* and Other Pro-MRND Newspapers

In addition to the independent press, which struggled to develop despite widespread restrictions and took risks in reporting human rights abuses, another press soon emerged which enjoyed official backing and appears to have served as a mouthpiece for members of the *Akazu*. It was in these organs, rather than in the independent press, that overt hate speech against Tutsi became so systematic as to seem the norm.[1] The first, and most notorious, was *Kangura* newspaper, noted for its systematic and virulent abuse of Tutsi, as illustrated by its notorious "10 Hutu Commandments" (see page 67). The newspaper appears to have been established by officials to counter the influence of the popular *Kanguka*. Even in its choice of titles, the newspaper presented itself as a self-conscious imitation of *Kanguka*; both titles mean "Wake up!" in Kinyarwanda, and sound similar. However, *Kangura*'s very different orientation was clear from its slogan, "*ijwi rigamije gukangura no kurengera rubanda nyamwinshi*", which means, "the voice which seeks to awaken and defend the 'majority people'".

Kangura was first published in May 1990, the same month that *Kanguka* Director, Valens Kajeguhakwa, was placed under house arrest. The first number of issues of this newspaper contained vociferous attacks on him and on journalist Vincent Rwabukwisi. The May issue claimed that Rwabukwisi, a Hutu, was a "Tutsi serving the interests of his brothers who want to restore the monarchy". Another article was entitled "the double-dealing of Kajeguhakwa which backfired". The June issue, featured a second piece on Kajeguhakwa, claiming that he represented the Tutsi. It alleged that they controlled 70 per cent of the country's wealth but were ungrateful about the assistance which it claimed the Rwandan government had provided them. Instead, *Kangura* maintained, the Tutsi aimed to overthrow the Republic and reintroduce a feudal monarchy, insinuating prior knowledge of the RPF invasion which was to take place just one month later.[2] The following month, Vincent Rwabukwisi was detained. (See Chapter 3, section 2, page 53.)

Later in 1990, Hassan Ngeze, Editor-in-Chief of *Kangura*, was detained and charged with subversion after the publication of his article claiming that the Tutsi enjoyed disproportionate wealth in Rwanda. On 22 October, he was sentenced to a two-year suspended sentence, whereas his colleague from *Kanguka*, Vincent Rwabukwisi, who was also tried the same month, received 15 years.[3] It is widely believed that charges were filed against Ngeze to make it appear that the authorities were not singling out *Kanguka*, particularly given that *Kangura* had openly applauded the repressive measures taken against Ngeze's more liberal counterpart.

Only one other incident occurred in which *Kangura* staff were censured by the authorities. On 4 August 1991, Hassan Ngeze was again briefly detained, following a complaint by the Burundian authorities, who were angered by reports in *Kangura* which claimed that the government of Burundi was providing military aid to the RPF. President Habyarimana is reported to have ordered Ngeze's immediate arrest as a means of appeasing Burundian President, Pierre Buyoya[4]. Three days later, Radio Rwanda reported on a meeting between Rwandan Foreign Minister Casimir Bizimungu and his Burundian counterpart in which the Rwandan Foreign Minister pointed to the recent arrest of Ngeze as proof that the Rwandan government was not backing the newspaper. The national radio station explained: "Mr [Casimir] Bizimungu insisted on clarifying an ambiguity [...] the *Kangura* newspaper was wrongly taken by some people as having governmental allegiance. The evidence is that its editor-in-chief has been detained more than once".[5]

In contrast to their colleagues within the independent press, journalists at *Kangura* and other pro-MRND newspapers were rarely prosecuted, despite their constant breaches of the law. François-Xavier Nsanzuwera, former Public Prosecutor for Kigali, noted the level of impunity which Hassan Ngeze enjoyed by virtue of his relationship with high-level authorities. In a letter of 6 August 1991, to Sylvestre

Nsanzimana, then Minister of Justice, he explained that the Attorney-General had issued a written directive instructing the security forces not to arrest Hassan Ngeze. Meanwhile, *Kangura* staff were not subject to harassment by the MRND or CDR militias but, instead, were assisted by their party leaders. On 28 September 1992, for example, CDR leader Jean-Bosco Barayagwiza wrote to Amnesty International asking the organization to campaign on behalf of Hassan Ngeze, who had been arrested the previous month.[6] *Kangura* even appeared to enjoy the support of President Habyarimana who, when questioned in Paris on 24 April 1991 about the newspaper's excesses, argued that it was merely exercising the right to freedom of expression.[7]

Kangura is also reported to have enjoyed financial and logistical support from high-level officials. According to *Reporters sans frontières* (RSF), *Kangura* was principally financed by Félicen Kabuga, financial advisor to President Habyarimana and future President of the Board of Directors of RTLM. RSF also found that Joseph Nzirorera, future RTLM shareholder, with links to "Network Zero", as well as three members of the *Akazu*, Charles Nzabagerageza, Jean-Baptiste Nyabusore, the nephew of Juvénal Habyarimana, and Pierre Tegera, were behind *Kangura*.[8] Elie Sagatwa, another "Network Zero" leader, is also alleged to have supported the newspaper.[9] In addition, African Rights reported that Agathe Habyarimana, the President's wife, was involved in the publication.[10]

From April 1991 onwards, the newspaper, with a circulation of approximately 10,000, was printed free of charge by a national printing company, the *Imprimerie nationale*. Charles Uyisenga, manager at another state-owned printing house, *Edition à la Régie de l'Imprimerie scolaire*, stated that only about 1,000 to 3,000 copies of the newspaper were actually sold and that civil servants in Kigali and other major cities distributed the rest, free of charge.[11] François-Xavier Nsanzuwera reported to ARTICLE 19 that FAR Colonel Anatole Nsengiyumva, then head of military intelligence, personally assisted with the distribution of *Kangura* in the capital.[12]

Perhaps the most compelling indication of *Kangura*'s official connections was the content of the newspaper, which in many ways mirrored official rhetoric. The newspaper accused opposition parties of being divisive and of encouraging RPF attacks. Soon after the parties were formally registered in July 1991, a *Kangura* editorial stated: "If the Hutu continue to bicker amongst themselves, in different political parties, the *Inkotanyi* and their accomplices will exterminate us".[13] Opposition leaders were systematically attacked and ridiculed in *Kangura's* pages, which regularly depicted figures such as Prime Minister Agathe Uwilingiyimana and Faustin Twagiramungu of the MDR as naked caricatures, in a series of vulgar cartoons.[14]

Kangura refused to support initiatives to promote freedom of the press. On 23 May 1991, when several other newspapers published an open letter to the President to protest the repressive measures taken against the media, and even specifically mentioned the case against *Kangura*, Hassan Ngeze chose not to sign the petition. Instead, *Kangura* supported government officials in denying that human rights abuses were being committed in Rwanda.[15]

In line with the authorities, *Kangura* identified and denounced people whom it claimed were "enemies", "accomplices", and "traitors", secretly working for the RPF in Rwanda. In issue No. 7 of December 1990, *Kangura* published a list of 41 merchants in Kigali who were suspected of supporting the RPF, stating that it had received this information directly from the authorities.[16] Just as high-level officials accused the international media of conspiring with the RPF, so *Kangura* targeted individual foreign correspondents, alleging they were RPF agents. In issue No. 8 of January 1991, *Kangura* attacked Belgian journalist Marie-France Cros, of *La Libre Belgique*, in an article entitled, "Marie-France Cros' artful lies and her complicity with the *Inkotanyi*", after she had criticized *Kangura's* racist content in her articles and in broadcasts for Deutsche Welle.[17] The newspaper also repeated calls by the authorities for people to be vigilant and to participate in repulsing the RPF attack. It warned: "Let us learn about the *Inkotanyi* plans and then let us exterminate every last one of them".[18]

Given the context of widespread arrests and state-sponsored violence against civilians, under the pretext of security, it was clearly intimidating to be publicly accused of supporting the rebels. Yet for people who were denounced by the newspaper, the consequences often proved more tangible. Shortly after denunciation, many of *Kangura's* scapegoats were persecuted by governmental authorities. Even government officials were not immune. In issue No. 7, *Kangura* declared that the government was infiltrated by "accomplices of the enemy" and urged the President to confront this problem. On its front cover, the newspaper published the names and photographs of six high-level government officials who, it claimed, were working for the RPF: François Habyakare, *Ministre de la Fonction Publique* (Civil Service Minister); Théoneste Mujyanama, *Ministre de la Justice* (Minister of Justice); J M Mugemana, *Ministre de l'Intérieur* (Minister of the Interior); Antoine Ntashamaje, *Ministre des Relations Institutionnelles*;[19] Alphonse-Marie Nkubito, *Procureur Général près de la Cour d'Appel de Kigali* (Attorney-General for Kigali Appeals Court), and Bonaventure Habimana, *secrétaire général du MRND* (MRND Secretary-General). In February 1991, all four ministers were dismissed during a cabinet reshuffle. Alphonse-Marie Nkubito was punitively transferred from Kigali to a more remote area and Bonaventure Habimana was sidelined from the party leadership.[20]

In another case, Christophe Mfizi, Director of ORINFOR, was dismissed just a few days after *Kangura* published a letter to the editor complaining about him, supposedly from a reader in Gisenyi *préfecture*. After Ferdinand Nahimana was appointed to the post, *Kangura* ran a piece praising this decision:

> ... a *Kangura* reader has complained of the inad-
> equacy of the staff at Radio Rwanda. He has been
> heard. A new boss has been appointed to head
> ORINFOR and the first programmes are full of
> promise. This appointment was necessary to
> awaken a people under attack who remain asleep.
> Bravo Radio Rwanda!![21]

This passage appears all the more dubious since it does not refer to any specific or plausible complaint which might have been made about Mfizi. Instead, the newspaper applauds Nahimana's nomination, without reference to any changes he is expected to make at ORINFOR.

Whatever *Kangura* called for usually occurred, when it related to specific individuals, and this added to the fear which the newspaper inspired. This correlation between what was published and what later followed, appears to have stemmed from the newspaper's relationship with *Akazu* members, rather than from any independent influence which the newspaper actually enjoyed. François-Xavier Nsanzuwera told

The Rise of "Hate Media"

ARTICLE 19 that he read *Kangura* and paid attention if the newspaper called for something specific to happen or made a prediction. But, he explained, there was nothing magical about this: "I believed it [what was threatened or predicted by *Kangura*], not because they [the people behind *Kangura*] were prophets, but because they were the ones who carried it out [the threatened action]".

These attacks on individuals did not technically constitute incitement, but were an indication that certain people would soon be targeted by the authorities, almost a preview of what the authorities were planning next. Beyond predicting and applauding the government's persecution of Tutsi and Hutu moderates, however, *Kangura* urged its readers to discriminate against these groups. In this role, *Kangura* engaged in incitement to hatred, presented at its crudest in the form of the "10 Hutu Commandments", which mimic the 10 Commandments of the Bible, well-known throughout this predominantly Christian country. Published in December 1990, these "Commandments" were instructions to mistreat and discriminate against Tutsi. *Kangura* attempted to justify these measures by claiming that all Tutsi were dangerous and aimed to exterminate Hutu, suggesting that they must be dealt with before they could strike. The "10 Commandments" were presented as a response to an earlier article published in *Kangura*, entitled the *"Plan de colonisation Tutsi"* ("Tutsi colonization plan"), a clearly fictitious account about how, supposedly, the Tutsi were planning to colonize the entire region of Central Africa and enslave the Hutu. *Kangura's* message echoed official government propaganda about the RPF:

> Since the Social Revolution of 1959, the Tutsi have never relinquished their plan to take over the country, to exterminate the intellectuals and to dominate the Hutu farmers.[22]

This statement was an implicit reference to the RPF invasion, which was always presented by the authorities as a plan by an ethnic minority to rule "the majority". While the Rwandan authorities exaggerated the size of the attack and the threat of the RPF itself, *Kangura* tried to persuade its readers that the rebel invasion was only one part of a larger plan by the Tutsi to "dominate" the Hutu.

The "Commandments" called upon Hutu not to trust any Tutsi, particularly women. They stigmatized Hutu who failed to discriminate against Tutsi, declaring that any Hutu who even conducts business with Tutsi is a "traitor". The "commandments" also supported the ethnic and regional quota system in schools, stating that the education sector should be dominated primarily by Hutu. Finally, *Kangura* declared that every Hutu must not only follow these commandments but also firmly believe in them and faithfully spread the word, by proselytizing. The "10 Hutu Commandments" conclude: "Every Muhutu must widely disseminate this ideology. Any Muhutu who persecutes his Muhutu brother for having read, spread and taught this ideology, is a traitor".[23]

Although *Kangura* was the most well-known example of government-sponsored hate propaganda, other "hate" newspapers demonstrated similar links with the Presidency. The other most striking example was the monthly magazine *Umurava*, founded in May 1991, which appears to have been created and financed by several prominent figures in the government and the military. According to its former Editor Janvier Afrika,[24] the newspaper's founders included President Habyarimana, Ferdinand Nahimana, and leading "Network Zero" members Joseph Nzirorera, Charles Nzabagerageza, Séraphin Rwabukumba and Capt. Pascal Simbikangwa. Tito Mongi, who had been working at Radio Rwanda, is reported to have been invited to join the newspaper by Ferdinand Nahimana.[25] These figures are believed to have retained editorial control over its content and to have used it to promote their ideas. The March 1992 issue of *Umurava* (No. 8) featured an interview with Capt. Simbikangwa, whose role in human rights abuses was well-known at the time.[26] Like *Kangura*, *Umurava* frequently sang the praises of the President: "It is God who gave Habyarimana the power to govern the country; He is the One who will show the President the way".[27]

In August 1992, two separate editions of *Umurava* issue No. 9 were published when Editor Janvier Afrika attempted to introduce greater independence in the magazine. His version criticized Capt. Simbikangwa and failed to follow the government line on the President and the *Akazu*. Meanwhile, the government-backed *Umurava* continued its pro-MRND editorial line much as before, declaring its strong support for President Habyarimana. Subsequently the govern-ment-sponsored *Umurava* was discontinued for reasons unknown.[28]

Some ten other newspapers emerged which also engaged in varying degrees of incitement to ethnic hatred and which are alleged to have received support from the Presidency.[29] Although less is known about their specific connections to officials, some were formally affiliated with the MRND or CDR, and all of them consistently promoted the ruling party in their articles. *Interahamwe*, an official MRND publication, edited by the *Interahamwe* militia leader Robert Kajuga, published virulent attacks on opposition party leaders.[30] After representatives of several opposition parties travelled to Brussels in mid-1992 to begin negotiations with the RPF, *Interahamwe* claimed that these individuals had betrayed their country and called upon its readers to apprehend them. It published an "Urgent Communiqué" which stated,

> The people are angry ... The people want security personnel to remain vigilant ... The people prom-ise a satisfactory reward to every person who arrests these traitors and hands them over to the authorities.[31]

This publication also announced schedules for forthcoming meetings organized by the MRND party and its militia. As the *Interahamwe* became stronger, individuals who risked attack often purchased the publication so they could be sure to leave the area in advance of the meetings or rallies.

La Médaille Nyiramacibiri, an extremist newspaper named after Dian Fossey, repeatedly incited ethnic hatred.[32] In September 1991, one month after information about the Bagogwe massacres had been made public, the newspaper denied that any Tutsi had been killed but instead claimed that the Bagogwe were responsible for widespread violence in north-west Rwanda:

> They are the ones [the Tutsi] who have sparked the violence in the Mutura region by provoking the population, beating and killing a soldier just as ... the *Inyenzi* had stepped up their attacks. ... the fury

of the Bagogwe is stronger than that of lions. ...
Why do certain Tutsi like blood?[33]

This passage not only insinuated that all the Tutsi in Rwanda collabo-
rated with the RPF, committing violence within the country while the
RPF intensified its attacks from Uganda, but also alleged they were
dangerous independently of their association with the RPF and were
inherently bloodthirsty. Reiterating the government's explanation of
these massacres, the article claimed that the Bagogwe had disappeared
because they left to join the RPF.

Like *Kangura*, *La Médaille Nyiramacibiri* intimidated independent journalists who reported on human rights abuses against Tutsi. In
September 1991, *Rwanda Rushya* journalist André Kameya received
an anonymous death threat, written on the official letterhead of the
Ministry of Defence.[34] This above-mentioned article from *La Médaille
Nyiramacibiri* reiterated the warning to Kameya and was written as if
personally addressed to the journalist, referring to him throughout the
article as "you".[35]

The newspaper attacked Kameya for his coverage of the Bagogwe
massacres. It accused him of "representing" the Tutsi and publishing
misinformation to protect them: "Kameya ... these Tutsi ... you
willingly defend, they have appointed you [to represent them] and trust
you, but you share their stupidity".[36] It claimed that his reporting on
the Bagogwe could plunge Rwanda into further violence. Referring to
figures which Kameya had published on the massacres, *La Médaille
Nyiramacibiri* stated: "this list, by its very nature, is likely to provoke
conflict between Rwanda's people".[37]

2   The Foundation of Radio-Télévision Libre des Mille Collines

Radio-Télévision Libre des Mille Collines (one thousand hills free
radio – RTLM), a nominally private radio station with informal
connections to high-level government officials and members of the
Akazu, was added to the other government-sponsored "hate" media in
mid-1993. The idea of creating an independent radio station, devoted

entirely to the agenda of extremists within the MRND, appears to have arisen in response to reforms at Radio Rwanda, which had been under pressure from opposition parties to grant them access since late 1991.[38] Plans to establish RTLM were discussed tentatively in 1991 when, reportedly, preliminary meetings were arranged by Ferdinand Nahimana, Jean-Bosco Barayagwiza, Stanislas Simbizi and Télesphore Bizimungu, who were later to become founding shareholders.[39] In May 1991, one month before the legalization of opposition parties, *Kangura* published a report which claimed that a private radio station would begin broadcasting from Gisenyi *préfecture*, using an FM frequency, on 1 July 1991.[40]

Moves to found RTLM were finally initiated after Ferdinand Nahimana was dismissed from ORINFOR in April 1992 when the position of Minister of Information was allocated to an opposition party in the transitional coalition government (see Chapter 6, section 1). Attempted reforms by the new Minister of Information, Pascal Ndengejeho, became a source of strife for CDR leaders, who claimed that Radio Rwanda was unfairly dominated by left-wing opposition parties. In a CDR rally on 18 October 1992, organized to protest against the transitional coalition government and its peace negotiations with the RPF, militants shouted "Free Radio Rwanda!" as one of their main demonstration slogans.[41]

Radio-Télévision Libre des Mille Collines, Société Anonyme (RTLM, SA), was established as a jointly founded company with 50 original shareholders and was officially registered on 8 April 1993. Although RTLM began to broadcast on 8 July 1993, the official contract between the government and the radio station was only later signed on 30 September by Minister of Information Faustin Rucogoza and Félicien Kabuga, on behalf of RTLM.[42] Another procedural irregularity occurred in the application of the terms of registration. Article 13 of the Statutes specified that the radio station was required to be managed by a Board of Directors, composed of between five and nine members nominated by RTLM's General Assembly, which included all 50 of the original shareholders plus all other shareholders of the station. The Board of Directors was responsible for electing the President and Vice-President of the Board, who would be legally responsible for all matters relating to the station. However, individuals involved with RTLM report that the Board of Directors was never appointed, although Félicien Kabuga, financial adviser to President Habyarimana, served from the beginning as President of the Board of Directors. Instead of a Board which would be accountable to all donors and founding shareholders, RTLM was run by an informal commission, composed of several individuals, led by Ferdinand Nahimana who, by all accounts, was the driving force behind the project.

Founders: links with the militias and interim government

The 50 original shareholders were, for the most part, extremely prominent figures, ranging from bank managers and businessmen, to journalists in the official media, army officers and government officials (see Appendix). Of the 50 individuals, 40 were from the north (17 from Ruhengeri *préfecture*, 16 from Gisenyi and seven from Byumba), President Habyarimana's region, whose elite dominated the inner circles of power. Many had close personal ties with members of the *Akazu* or with the President himself, often through business or marriage. Félicien Kabuga was an in-law to the President; his daughter Bernadette was married to Jean-Pierre Habyarimana, the President's son. Ernest Buroko was the protégé of Protais Zigiranyirazo, brother of Agathe Habyarimana. Alphonse Ntirivamunda is the son-in-law of the President.[43] Radio Rwanda journalist Robert Simba is the son of Aloys Simba, a retired colonel who played an important role in the *coup d'état* which brought President Habyarimana to power.

Most of the founders belonged to the MRND or CDR. Several served as spokespersons or high-profile leaders for these parties, such as CDR leader Jean-Bosco Barayagwiza, member of the CDR Executive Central Committee Stanislas Simbizi, and Ferdinand Nahimana, who reportedly led CDR rallies although, officially, he was a member of the MRND. In 1996 the latter was indicted by the International Criminal Tribunal for Rwanda and detained in Cameroon. As of 1 September 1996 he was still awaiting transfer to Arusha. Jean Habyarimana, a civil engineer, was the President of the MRND for the city of Kigali. Joseph Nzirorera, former Minister of Public Works and close contact of the President, was the Secretary-General for the MRND. In addition, singer Simon Bikindi, whose anti-Tutsi song, "*Je déteste ces Hutu*" ("I hate these Hutu"), was repeatedly played at CDR rallies and on RTLM but banned from Radio Rwanda, was also among the original 50 shareholders.

Beyond their regional, political or ideological affiliations, the founders are noticeable for the key positions which many of them held in the government, both before April 1994 and throughout the genocide. In some cases, this meant that they were well-placed to assist RTLM with practical issues. For example, Joseph Serugendo, who had long worked as the Head of Technical Services at ORINFOR, is alleged to have provided free technical services to RTLM, which does not appear to have employed its own technicians.[44] André Ntagerura, member of the MRND central committee, was Minister of Transport and Communications before and during the genocide; this Ministry is responsible for granting and allocating frequencies to radio stations.

Others held important posts, were generally influential, and could rely on a large network of supporters. Télesphore Bizimungu was the Director-General of the Ministry of Planning, which allocated not only project money from donors but also scholarships and grants, which, in principle, were supposed to be handled by the Ministry of Education.[45] At the time of President Habyarimana's death, CDR leader Jean-Bosco Barayagwiza was the Director of Political Affairs at the Ministry of Foreign Affairs. He had earlier worked as the *Directeur de Cabinet* for a former Secretary-General of the Organization of African Unity.[46] Charles Nzabagerageza, another powerful individual, was alleged by the International Commission of Investigation to have been involved in the massacre of the Bagogwe.[47]

In many instances, these figures appear to have formed part of the "second power" which imposed itself through "Network Zero" and the militias; some reportedly occupied positions of leadership in these paramilitary organizations. Déogratias Nsabimana, Chief-of-Staff of the Armed Forces, who later died with President Habyarimana in the plane crash of 6 April 1994, was alleged by his relative Jean Birara, former governor of the Central Bank, to have possessed, in February 1994, a list of 1,500 names of people in Kigali to be killed.[48] Georges Rutaganda, who served as Second National Vice-President of the *Interahamwe*, was indicted in 1996 by the International Criminal Tribunal for Rwanda[49] on eight charges, including distributing weapons to militia members in Kigali immediately following the plane crash on 6 April. He was scheduled to face trial on 17 October 1996.[50] African Rights reported that Phéneas Ruhumuliza, a businessman close to Georges Rutaganda, was First National Vice-President of the *Interahamwe*.[51] Alphonse Ntirivamunda, Director-General in the Ministry of Public Works before 6 April 1994 and son-in-law of President Habyarimana, was identified by Professor Filip Reyntjens as one of the principal leaders of "Network Zero", in October 1992.[52] Officials in his Ministry are believed to have recruited *Interahamwe* members among the workers whom they employed for short-term projects, such as road repairs and other manual work. Charles Nzabagerageza is also believed to have played an important role in "Network Zero", and was a suspect in the assassination attempt on the former Rwandan Ambassador to Rome in January 1994, who was the target of a grenade attack in Kigali shortly after he resigned from the MRND party.[53]

A significant number of the original 50 RTLM shareholders held formal positions in, or were active in publicly supporting, the self-proclaimed interim government which took power on 8 April 1994. Jean-Bosco Barayagwiza continued to act as Director of Political Affairs at the Ministry of Foreign Affairs and during the genocide played a leading role in representing the government internationally. Along with Foreign Minister Jérôme Bicamumpaka, Barayagwiza held meetings with President François Mitterrand, Prime Minister Edouard Balladur and Foreign Minister Alain Juppé in France and travelled to the UN headquarters in New York.[54] After the genocide began in April 1994, Félicien Kabuga created and headed a "Provisional Committee" to mobilize people in support of the interim government. He also called upon Rwandans to respect and value what he described as the "bravery and sacrifice" of the armed forces in "persecuting the enemy and his people".[55]

Meanwhile, André Ntagerura was retained as Minister of Transport and Communications and is alleged by African Rights to have assisted in planning the killings in Karengera *commune* during the genocide.[56] On 16 August 1996, he was indicted by the International Criminal Tribunal for Rwanda, which requested that he be sent to Arusha, Tanzania, from Cameroon, where he had been detained since March. Augustin Ngirabatware, from the MDR "Hutu

Power" movement, also continued as Minister for Public Works. After 6 April, Alphonse Ntirivamunda maintained his position of Director-General of roads and bridges in the Ministry of Public Works. Journalist Froduald Ntawulikura also continued to work at Radio Rwanda during this period and, according to *Reporters sans frontières*, is reported to have incited genocide.[57] Charles Nzabagerageza was employed as *conseiller* in the Ministry of Transport and Communications.[58] Others changed positions or were promoted during the genocide. In mid-June, after the interim government had relocated to Gisenyi from Gitarama, Joseph Nzirorera, Secretary-General of the MRND and former Minister of Public Works, was nominated President of Parliament. Radio Rwanda journalist Jean-Baptiste Bamwanga was appointed Director of ORINFOR after Jean-Marie Vianney Higiro was forced to flee.

In addition, RTLM shareholder Pasteur Musabe, Director-General of the *Banque Continentale Africaine du Rwanda* (BACAR), a prestigious private bank, was arrested by the Cameroonian authorities in 1996 in connection with the 1994 genocide. He is the younger brother of Colonel Théoneste Bagasora, who is reported to have played a central role in arming the militias since 1991 and is believed to have been involved in the orchestration of the genocide on a national level.[59] In March 1996, Bagasora was arrested in Cameroon on the basis of an international arrest warrant issued by Belgium for the killings of the 10 Belgian UNAMIR troops on 7 April. On 16 August 1996, he was indicted by the International Criminal Tribunal for Rwanda. As of 1 September 1996 he had not yet been sent to Arusha.

Shareholders who financed RTLM

The founders of RTLM mounted a massive campaign to solicit funding for the radio station, which required a minimum capital of Rwfr3 million (US$17,836) in order to operate (Statutes, Article 36).[60]

Although the radio station appears to have relied on large investments from a few key individuals who supported the project from its inception, such as Félicien Kabuga and Séraphin Rwabukumba, brother-in-law of the President, its founders aimed to solicit smaller investments from a much wider section of people, through donations and membership (Article 6), with a target figure of Rwfr100 million (US$594,530). A minimum of Rwfr5,000 (US$30) was required in order to become a shareholder and participate in the General Assemblies which were held periodically to review matters relating to the radio station.

The fund-raising campaign appears to have begun only after April 1993, once the station had been formally registered. Several observers reported that Radio Rwanda broadcast a communiqué in July 1993 announcing the creation of RTLM and appealing for people to invest in the project. RTLM supporters even lobbied Rwandans living in Europe for investment. During the summer of 1993, Joseph Désiré Ruhigira, a retired army officer living in France, along with Paulin Murayi, MRND representative for Belgium, and Papias Ngaboyamahina, a student, approached numerous Rwandans in Belgium for funding.[61] Ruhigira also circulated an open letter which stated that RTLM aimed to counter the problem of lack of information in Rwanda:

> It has proven necessary and urgent to set up an organ which can not only present opposing viewpoints ... but also serve in the fight for democracy and the defence of republicanism.[62]

The letter also noted that RTLM accepted contributions from foreign nationals as well as from Rwandans.

The total amount of funds raised by RTLM and the number of people who donated money is unknown; it is believed that money was deposited into several bank accounts in Europe and in Rwanda. ARTICLE 19 has obtained unconfirmed details of an alleged account in the *Banque Commerciale* in Kigali where people deposited money for RTLM. According to this information, 218 people deposited money into the account between 29 April 1993 and 17 February 1994. The deposits amounted to a total of Rwfr1,958,400 (US$11,643) Although information was not available about all of the investors, the list includes a number of well-known names. Three of the largest investors listed are believed to have played significant roles in the genocide. Augustin Bizimana, Minister of Defence during the interim government, invested Rwfr100,000 (US$595) on 22 July 1993. Capt.

Pascal Simbikangwa, a leading member of "Network Zero", also invested a total of Rwfr100,000 (US$595); he deposited Rwfr70,000 (US$416) on 10 July 1993 and Rwfr30,000 (US$178) on 10 August 1993. Alphonse Higaniro, who invested Rwfr100,000 (US$595), was arrested in Belgium on charges of genocide. Two others who also invested Rwfr100,000 (US$595), Jean Claude Ndamiye and André Muvunyi, could not be traced by ARTICLE 19. The vast majority of the donors to this account, 207 out of 218, invested much smaller amounts, between Rwfr5,000 (US$30) and Rwfr20,000 (US$119).

The list also includes Major-General Augustin Bizimungu, Commander-in-Chief of the FAR after 6 April 1994, who replaced Déogratias Nsabimana after he was killed in the plane crash. André Rwamakuba, a member of the MDR "Hutu Power" movement, who was appointed Minister of Primary Education in the interim government of April 1994, invested Rwfr5,000 (US$30) in RTLM on 4 May 1993.

RTLM journalists

RTLM employed eight journalists, most of whom were highly experienced. All of them had previously worked for the government media or with pro-MRND newspapers and are believed to have been members of the MRND or CDR. Gaspard Gahigi, Editor-in-Chief of RTLM, received his *licence* (Masters degree) at the *Institut des Sciences et Techniques de Communication.*[63] Before working at RTLM, he served in two high-level positions at ORINFOR, first as head of the Press Service and then as head of the Radio Service between 1979-1985. During this period, he worked simultaneously as an Agence France-Presse (AFP) correspondent.[64] After moving to Togo, he worked for a newspaper from 1987 to 1990, and then returned to Rwanda and founded the MRND party newspaper, *Umurwanashyaka.*

Kantano Habimana, who is considered to have been one of the most popular announcers at RTLM, also had considerable journalistic experience. He studied in St Petersburg, where he obtained a Masters degree in Journalism, and later worked at the government newspaper *Imvaho* and at *Umurwanashyaka.*[65] Habimana also founded a newspaper, *Shishoza* ("Be Discerning"), which produced only five issues. Earlier, he had served as a local MRND leader in Butare, his region of origin.

Noël Hitimana, another well-known RTLM figure, brought with him a long experience of radio broadcasting. He had worked at Radio Rwanda for several years before being sacked, reportedly because of chronic alcoholism. At RTLM, he openly joked about his heavy drinking, a particularly taboo subject in Rwanda, and often went on the air obviously intoxicated, to the point where he sometimes had difficulty speaking clearly.

Valérie Bemeriki was also a prominent personality at RTLM. Unlike many of her contemporaries, she did not attend university but had previously worked on MRND party papers, *Umurwanashyaka* and *Interahamwe*, before being recruited by RTLM.

Another notorious RTLM figure was Georges Ruggiu, a teacher and Belgian national of Italian origin, who later evaded arrest in a refugee camp in Tanzania in mid-1995. He apparently became involved with hardliners in the Rwandan community in Belgium a few years before RTLM was created. He is believed to have been introduced to RTLM's founders by the then MRND representative for Belgium, Paulin Murayi. Georges Ruggiu, along with the Zairean Philippe Mbirizi, about whom little is known, conducted French-language broadcasts for the station. Georges Ruggiu is reported to have led the anti-Belgian and anti-UNAMIR campaign on RTLM.

Journalist Ananie Nkurunziza had previously worked as editor-in-chief of the newspaper *Intera*, which was founded in 1989 by leading "Network Zero" member Séraphin Rwabukumba. In addition, he is reported to have formerly worked for the Rwandan Intelligence Service, based in Uganda.[66] Emmanuel Rucogoza, a younger and less well-known journalist, came to RTLM after a brief but unsuccessful stint at Radio Rwanda.

Notes

[1] For an overview of the content of this "hate press," see J-P Chrétien, *Rwanda: Les médias du génocide* (Paris: Éditions Karthala, 1995). This book presents a volume of excerpts from *Kangura* and other newspapers, from 1990-1994, translated from Kinyarwanda into French.

[2] *Kangura*, No. 3 (June 1990), as quoted in J-P Chrétien, "'Presse Libre' et propagande raciste au Rwanda: Kangura et 'les 10 commandements du Hutu'", in *Politique Africaine*, No. 42 (Paris: June 1991), 111.

[3] Committee to Protect Journalists, *Attacks on the Press 1990* (New York: CPJ, 1991), 100.

[4] Pierre Buyoya served as President of Burundi from 1987-1993 and, on 25 July 1996, seized power in a *coup d'état*.

[5] Radio Rwanda, Kigali (French), 0430 GMT, 7 Aug. 1991, "Rwandan and Burundian Foreign Ministers Discuss 'Orchestrated' Rwandan Media", in *BBC Summary of World Broadcasts*, 9 Aug. 1991.

[6] F Reyntjens, "Akazu, 'Escadrons de la mort' et autres 'Réseau zéro': un historique des résistances au changement politique depuis 1990, in A Guichaoua (ed.), *Les crises politiques au Burundi et au Rwanda (1993-1994)* (Lille/Paris: Université des Sciences et Technologies/Éditions Karthala, 1995), 271.

[7] J-P Chrétien, "Media and Propaganda in Preparation for and During the Rwandan Genocide," study submitted to UNESCO by *Reporters sans frontières* and produced in collaboration with the Centre de Recherches Africaines (Paris 1-CNRS) (Paris: UNESCO, 30 April 1995), 9.

[8] Reporters sans frontières, *Rwanda: médias de la haine ou presse démocratique? Rapport de mission 16-24 Sept. 1994* (Paris: RSF, 1994), 19.

[9] F Misser, "Rwanda: médias et génocide", *Le Monde Diplomatique*, Aug. 1994.

[10] African Rights, *Death, Despair and Defiance*, Revised Edition (London: African Rights, 1995), 101.

[11] Chrétien, note 1 above, at 31.

[12] In 1996 Colonel Anatole Nsengiyumva was indicted by the International Criminal Tribunal for Rwanda on charges relating to the 1994 genocide, and detained in Cameroon. As of 1 Sept. 1996 he was still awaiting transfer to Arusha, Tanzania.

[13] "Si les Hutu continuent à se chamailler dans différents partis politiques, les *Inkotanyi* et leurs complices vont nous exterminer". *Kangura*, No. 15 (Kigali: July 1991).

[14] Chrétien, note 1 above.

[15] See, for example, "Aucun massacre de Bagogwe ni Kinigi, ni ailleurs dans le nord du Rwanda", *Kangura*, no. 24 (Kigali: Sept. 1991), 19.

[16] Chrétien, note 2 above, at 114.

[17] "L'art de mentir de Marie-France Cros et sa complicité avec les *Inkotanyi*", ibid., at 112.

[18] "Apprenons à connaître les plans des *Inkotanyi* et prévoyons de les exterminer jusqu'au dernier". *Kangura*, no. 9 (Kigali: Feb. 1991), 10.

[19] A now defunct ministry which reviewed draft laws proposed in parliament to ensure they were in conformity with the Constitution.

[20] Chrétien, note 2 above, at 114.

[21] "Un lecteur de *Kangura* s'était plaint de la carence du personnel de Radio Rwanda. Il a été entendu. Un nouveau patron a été nommé à la tête de l'ORINFOR et les premières émissions de Radio Rwanda sont riches de promesses. C'est nécessaire pour réveiller un peuple agressé et qui dort. Radio Rwanda, Bravo!!". Chrétien, note 1 above, at 50.

[22] "Depuis la révolution sociale de 1959, pas un seul jour les Tutsi n'ont lâché l'idée de reconquérir le pouvoir et exterminer les intellectuels et dominer les agriculteurs Hutu". As cited in Chrétien, note 1 above, at 39.

[23] "Tout Muhutu doit diffuser largement la présente idéologie. Est traître tout Muhutu qui persécutera son frère Muhutu pour avoir lu, diffusé et enseigné cette idéologie". C Braeckman, *Rwanda: Histoire du génocide* (Paris: Editions Fayard, 1994), 140.

[24] He worked as a government informant and then in the "Information and Propaganda Service" in the Office of the Presidency before becoming a dissident.

[25] Chrétien, note 1 above, at 42-43.

[26] F Reyntjens, *L'Afrique des Grands Lacs en crise: Rwanda, Burundi: 1988-1994* (Paris: Éditions Karthala, 1994), 172.

[27] "C'est Dieu qui a donné à Habyarimana le pouvoir de diriger le pays, c'est lui qui indiquera la marche à suivre". Chrétien, note 1 above, at 46.

[28] Reyntjens, note 26 above, at 172.

[29] According to Jean-Pierre Chrétien and *Reporters sans frontières*, the following publications were all created by members of the *Akazu* in 1991: *Ijisho rya rubanda, Umurwanashyaka, La Victoire-turatsinze, Dusanasane imitima tudahushura, l'Echo des mille collines, La Médaille Nyiramacibiri, Kamarampaka, Jyambere, Kangura version internationale*. In addition, *Ijambo*, which began as an independent paper, later supported the "Hutu Power" movement and is believed to have been backed by the Presidency.

Chrétien, note 1 above, at 45-47.

[30] Ibid., at 52.

[31] "Le peuple est en colère ... Le peuple demande aux organes chargés de la securité de rester vigilants. ... Le peuple promet à toute personne qui arrêtera et mettra entre les mains des autorités ces traîtres une récompense qui lui donnera satisfaction". *Interahamwe*, no. 6 (25 June 1992), 5. As quoted in Chrétien, note 1 above, at 255.

[32] Dian Fossey was an American anthropologist, who studied gorillas in northern Rwanda. The slogan of the newspaper was a gorilla between two volcanoes.

[33] "Ce sont eux [les Tutsi] qui ont déclenché la violence dans la région de Mutura en provoquant la population, en frappant et en tuant un soldat à un moment où ... les *Inyenzi* avaient redoublé d'ardeur dans leurs attaques. ... la fureur des Bagogwe est plus forte que celle des lions. ... Pourquoi certains Tutsi aiment-ils le sang?" Georges Nkunzurwanda, "Kameya s'est fait le porte-parole des Tutsi", *La Médaille Nyiramacibiri*, no. 3 (Sept. 1991), 14-15. As quoted in Chrétien, note 1 above, at 176.

[34] It stated: "For having provoked the Rwandan Armed Forces ... To have taken the tolerance of the Rwandan People for a weakness; ... For being dangerous to the Rwandan people; You are condemned to death. We are going to kill you." As quoted in Committee to Protect Journalists, *Attacks on the Press in 1991* (New York: CPJ, 1992), 51.

[35] André Kameya was later killed during the 1994 genocide.

[36] "Kameya ... ces Tutsi dont tu te fais volontiers défenseur, ils t'ont délégué et ils t'accordent leur confiance, mais tu partages leurs sottises".

[37] "Cette liste de Kameya est de nature à provoquer des troubles et des conflits entre les enfants du Rwanda".

[38] Although several applications for private radio stations were made around the same period, RTLM was the only station granted a licence.

[39] According to journalist Sixbert Musangamfura, cited in Reporters sans frontières, note 8 above.

[40] *Kangura*, no. 16 (Kigali: July 1991).

[41] G Prunier, *The Rwanda Crisis 1959-1994: History of a Genocide* (London and New York: Hurst & Company and Columbia University Press, 1995), 164.

[42] *Convention d'Etablissement et d'Exploitation de Radiodiffusion ou de*

Télévision (Convention on the Establishment and the Operation of Radio and Television).

[43] Misser, note 9 above.

[44] RTLM is also believed to have been provided with free electricity. Chrétien, note 7 above, at 13.

[45] In 1996, Télesphore Bizimungu was arrested in Cameroon but, as of 1 September 1996 had not been indicted by the International Criminal Tribunal for Rwanda.

[46] African Rights, note 10 above, at 108.

[47] Fédération internationale des droits de l'homme, Africa Watch, Union interafricaine des droits de l'homme et des peuples, Centre international des droits de la personne et du développement démocratique, *Report of the International Commission of Investigation on Human Rights Violations in Rwanda since October 1, 1990 (7-21 Jan. 1993)* (New York: Human Rights Watch/Africa, March 1993), 23.

[48] Prunier, note 41 above, at 222.

[49] The International Criminal Tribunal for Rwanda was created by the UN Security Council (Resolution No. 955) on 8 Nov. 1994, and has its seat in Arusha, Tanzania. Resolution 955 provides for prosecution of those responsible for genocide, other violations of humanitarian law in Rwanda and neighbouring states in 1994. Its jurisdiction covers crimes occurring between 1 Jan. and 31 Dec. 1994.

[50] "Rwanda Genocide Trial Hears First 2 Suspects", *New York Times*, 31 May 1996.

[51] African Rights, note 10 above, at 163.

[52] Prunier, note 41 above, at 168.

[53] According to former Public Prosecutor François-Xavier Nsanzuwera, the case was never resolved.

[54] Prunier, note 41 above, at 277.

[55] As quoted in African Rights, note 10 above, at 110.

[56] Ibid., at 107.

[57] Reporters sans frontières, *Rwanda: l'impasse. La liberté de la presse après le génocide, 4 juillet 1994-28 aôut 1995* (Paris: Reporters sans frontières, 1995), 32-33.

[58] *Conseiller* is the third most powerful position in this Ministry, after the *Ministre* and *Directeur-Général*, respectively.

[59] African Rights, note 10 above, at 112.

[60] In 1993 168.2 Rwandan franc (Rwfr)=US$1. This exchange rate has been used throughout.

[61] Braeckman, note 23 above, at 163.

[62] "Il s'avère donc nécessaire et urgent de mettre sur pied un organe qui puisse non seulement donner une information contradictore ... mais aussi servir de combat pour la démocratie et la défense de l'institution républicaine". Braeckman, ibid.

[63] Chrétien, note 1 above, at 71.

[64] Reporters sans frontières, note 8 above.

[65] Chrétien, note 1 above, at 71.

[66] Ibid.

Chapter 5

RTLM BEFORE THE GENOCIDE
(8 July 1993–April 1994)

1   Western-style Radio Talk Show

> The question of Radio Mille Collines propaganda
> is a difficult one. There were so many genuinely
> silly things being said on the station, so many
> obvious lies, that it was hard to take seriously. It
> was like relying on the *National Enquirer* [a US
> supermarket tabloid] to determine your policy in
> outer space.
>
> *Lucie Edwards, Canadian Ambassador*[1]

RTLM broadcasts received little attention from the international community until the genocide, when the station's broadcasters were widely reported to have uttered macabre calls to violence such as, "the grave is only half full, who will help us to fill it?"[2] Allegations that RTLM constantly flaunted gory details of the killings during the genocide have led some observers to conclude that the station was simply morbid, and must have been so from its inception. This is an inaccurate and simplistic portrayal of a radio station which was far more subtle, and less direct, than most observers have acknowledged.

In its presentation and format, RTLM essentially resembled, and probably modelled itself after, Western-style radio talk shows, complete with audience participation, offensive jokes and popular music. In a country where both the official media and the rebel radio station were notoriously formal, the more entertaining RTLM faced no serious competition. RTLM was frequently listened to by a wide section of Kigali's population, including by office workers during working hours. Outside Kigali and other urban centres, the station is reported to have attracted people from urban backgrounds, administrators and teachers, rather than peasants from rural areas.

RTLM Before the Genocide

Sources close to the RPF claim that RTLM was extremely popular with the rebel soldiers, who clearly preferred it to Radio Muhabura, which constantly relayed RPF propaganda and was rather amateurish. Even Alexis Kanyarengwe, RPF President, is reported to have been an avid listener and, before the genocide, is said to have found the station very amusing.

Although RTLM has been described by some sources as a "professional" radio station[3], its broadcasters did not provide factual news reports or engage in standard journalistic activities, such as reporting items of public interest, or conducting field investigations. Instead, they presented informal and unstructured commentaries on various subjects, usually in the form of dialogues, and relied on lengthy interviews with guests to fill airtime. They also introduced the modern concept of audience participation, broadcasting RTLM's studio phone number and frequently inviting listeners to phone in with their comments. Broadcasters often relayed messages from listeners or referred to conversations they had had with individuals who called the station.

Given the level of RTLM broadcasters' professional experience, their decision to adopt Western style disc jockey personas appears to have been deliberate. In a conference paper presented in March 1994, RTLM Editor-in-Chief Gaspard Gahigi claimed that Radio Rwanda's formal and outmoded language was a major reason for its lack of impact on the Rwandan population. According to Gahigi, Rwandans were "poorly informed" because the "official media has ... retained its traditional rhetoric".[4] In contrast, RTLM broadcasters spent airtime joking around, rather than presenting serious programmes and, as a result, they quickly became familiar and sometimes comic figures, household names to many of their listeners.

The heavy drinking for which Noël Hitimana apparently lost his position at Radio Rwanda became an asset at RTLM, where he went on air directly after drinking sprees. His alcoholism also provided material for jokes which were certain to shock many listeners. On 3 April 1994, Hitimana, who used his diminutive nickname, Noheli, comically recounted how he had made light of his drinking with a listener who, supposedly, telephoned to ask why he was always in such a "good mood". Hitimana light-heartedly explained:

> Someone just called me and asked, 'Noheli, why
> are you always in such a good mood, what
> happened? ... I suspect that you have 'exorcized
> the evil spirit' my friend', ha! ... And I replied that
> it was just a matter of drinking tea, child of my
> mother, except that sugar has become impossible
> to find.[5]

On many occasions, the banter in RTLM's broadcasts was crude.
Earlier in the same broadcast, Hitimana, notorious for his vulgarity,
had made a comment which drew an analogy to the act of passing
wind: "People say ... 'if you're going to fart ... it should stink'. The
best thing to do is to produce a really foul smell".[6]

This type of language, far from having universal appeal, clearly
shocked and offended many listeners, but served to attract a specific
section of the population who were to form its most avid fans: young
people and delinquents. In an interview with ARTICLE 19, French
historian Gérard Prunier commented:

> RTLM was geared to people on street corners — if
> it was beamed to peasants, it was for the young
> ones. Their parents would have disapproved. It was
> for 20-year-olds and under. ... RTLM's target was
> gangs, young thugs.

This was an important audience to reach as young, destitute people
formed the vast majority of militia members, with the exception of
high-ranking leaders, who tended to be older and part of the elite. This
was a group which had not been greatly impressed by the standard
government propaganda about the RPF and Tutsi, which was largely
based on obscure references to the supposed evils of the Tutsi
monarchy which ruled before the 1959 Social Revolution. According
to Prunier:

> The older message was 'we need to set things right
> after they went wrong under the feudal monarchy'.
> The younger generation did not care about this. It
> meant nothing to them. ... you have to get the

support of people not yet born in the revolution of 1959. ... The ideas [of ethnic hatred against Tutsi] had been around for years. RTLM presented them in a form more palatable for the younger generation. RTLM used street language.

2   The Assassination of Melchior Ndadaye

From July to October 1993, RTLM broadcasts were reported to have been fairly innocuous, consisting mostly of popular music with little news or commentary. After the 21 October assassination of Melchior Ndadaye, the first democratically elected, and first Hutu President of Burundi, RTLM programmes quickly became inflammatory and began to incite ethnic hatred. Ndadaye and several members of his government were killed by a group of high-ranking officers of the mainly Tutsi Burundian Army who unsuccessfully attempted a *coup d'état*. Ndadaye's murder had a great impact on public opinion in Rwanda, where both the transition to democracy and the prospects for implementation of the Arusha Accords seemed increasingly fragile. RTLM used these events as a pretext to run ongoing commentaries for several weeks on the supposed dangers of the RPF, the Arusha Accords and the Tutsi generally.

RTLM broadcaster Kantano Habimana introduced one commentary on the events in Burundi by repeating a proverb which he claimed had been used by the extremist former Burundian Minister of the Interior in exile, Léonard Nyangoma:

> Even where the dog-eaters are few in number, they discredit the whole family. That proverb was used by ... Mr Nyangoma, meaning that those Burundian Tutsi thugs have killed democracy by torturing to death the elected President Ndadaye.[7]

This statement is clearly inflammatory, but Habimana presented it as an authoritative statement by citing the Burundian official as his source.

The political assassinations and coup attempt led to massive revenge killings of Tutsi civilians throughout Burundi. Security forces, who were principally Tutsi in origin, then conducted a brutal clampdown and committed atrocities against the Hutu population. In total, 50,000 deaths were reported, approximately 60 per cent Tutsi and 40 per cent Hutu, and 150,000 people were displaced by the violence.[8] Instead of focusing on the Burundian Army's role in the attempted coup and in the repression which followed, RTLM blamed both the assassinations and the massacres on the Tutsi generally. The station also failed to disclose the full extent of the atrocities, omitting information on the widespread violence against Tutsi, while exaggerating and distorting the abuses of Hutu. It also falsely alleged that the Burundian Army was shelling Gitega, the town where Ndadaye came from, "in the FRODEBU stronghold", in order to seek revenge for the killings of Tutsi.[9]

Furthermore, the radio station distorted the circumstances surrounding the killing of Ndadaye, who had been taken to a military camp and summarily executed, alleging that the coup plotters refused to turn over his remains. Habimana claimed:

> We have learned that Ndadaye's corpse was furtively buried, to hide the mutilations that those beasts have wrought on his body. Anyway, they will be accountable for this blood.[10]

According to one observer, RTLM even reported that this alleged refusal to hand over Ndadaye's corpse caused an international incident and that the government of Tanzania threatened military intervention to recover his body.

Although short of accurate information, RTLM announcers did not hesitate to draw sweeping conclusions in their commentaries on Burundi. The station tried to instil panic and fear by presenting events in Burundi as a threat to internal security in Rwanda, and called on listeners to intervene "on behalf" of the Hutu in Burundi, claiming that the violence would soon spread to Rwanda. An RTLM broadcaster quoted a headline from the newspaper *Ijambo* which criticized Hutu in Rwanda for failing to respond to the crisis in Burundi: "Ndadaye dies, the Hutu of Rwanda remain inactive".[11] He went on to read the article which supported military intervention in Burundi:

> The fact that the Rwandan army has not yet launched an attack on Burundi is a sad thing. They should go and destroy the quarters of *Inkotanyi* in Burundi, if they agree that the Hutu also have the right to live in Rwanda and Burundi. If they do not do that, the attack that will come from Burundi will be strong. To wait for the international community to go to the rescue of the Hutu in Burundi, is to delay too much, and this will allow the Tutsi to regroup.[12]

The *Ijambo* article, quoted in detail by RTLM without further commentary, twisted and purposely confounded developments in both countries. Instead of discussing the discrimination against Hutu and the lack of reform in the Burundian armed forces, RTLM presented the problems in Burundi as an extension of the Rwandan conflict with the RPF. Although the Arusha Accords had been signed in August 1993, the RPF was described as a continuing threat to regional security. RTLM claimed that the RPF, not the Burundian military, was behind the slaughter in Burundi. According to RTLM, the situation in Burundi required a military solution, outside intervention, rather than pressure for institutional reform from within. The FAR had to "destroy the quarters of *Inkotanyi* in Burundi, if they agree that the Hutu also have the right to live in Rwanda and Burundi".[13]

According to *Ijambo* and RTLM, the massacres of Hutu in Burundi were one phase in a larger plot to eliminate this ethnic group from the entire region. If Rwanda failed to take immediate action to ward off this looming threat, it would increase. *Ijambo*, as cited by RTLM, stated that sweeping measures were needed in order for the Hutu of Rwanda to succeed in defending themselves against this potential attack by "Tutsi": "All Rwandan Hutu are asked to contribute. Those who can use a gun, let them cross the border, those who cannot, let them learn, those who cannot yet, let them contribute money to buy guns and bullets".[14]

Meanwhile, RTLM openly equated the RPF with the Tutsi generally, in both Rwanda and Burundi, and claimed that failure to respond would "allow the Tutsi to regroup" and dominate the whole region. After these ambiguous calls to arms, RTLM proceeded to engage in clear attacks on Tutsi civilians in Rwanda and on RPF troops, claiming that all Hutu in Rwanda were equally moved by the death of Burundi's President and alleging that Rwandan Tutsi supported his killing. RTLM asserted: "After the coup in Burundi, all the Tutsi in Rwanda danced for joy, the Hutu of Rwanda were saddened".[15] In another broadcast, Kantano Habimana recounted how, supposedly, he had a conversation with a group of Tutsi Rwandans who declared themselves indifferent to the bloodshed in Burundi: "They asked me why I talk about them, why I want them to mourn for Burundi when they do not want to. I could not find anything to say".[16]

Meanwhile, RTLM used the events in Burundi as an excuse to denounce the Arusha Accords and to vilify the rebels. Although completely unconnected with the RPF, RTLM maintained that the coup attempt in Burundi represented a breach of the Rwanda peace agreement. Citing *Ijambo*, an RTLM broadcaster stated: "all Rwandans must understand that the Arusha Peace Accords are void". The broadcaster concluded that any peace agreement with the RPF would be inherently untenable because "[the decision] to give the Tutsi 40 per cent of the army was ended by the plan to overthrow the Hutu rule".[17] This was a critical allusion to the Arusha Accords which stipulated that the RPA would integrate with the FAR with a 40-60 per cent ratio. Moreover, Habimana accused UNAMIR, whose mandate was to oversee the implementation of the Accords, of working for the RPF:

> The RPF will ensure the security of its own lead-
> ers. Why cannot we take care of our own security
> and that of our leaders, while UNAMIR would
> watch those acting against the Peace Accord,
> instead of showing ... that they support the RPF ... .[18]

RTLM also broadcast false reports about RPF leaders, designed to instil fear about their presence in the country. Just after President Ndadaye's assassination, the station claimed that RPF President Alexis Kanyarengwe, a Hutu, had been killed by Tutsi soldiers from the RPA.

Habimana later reported that Kanyarengwe was still alive, but had been "shot when the coup in Burundi was taking place",[19] suggesting that he and the RPF had played a role in the putsch. The broadcaster falsely claimed that the RPF leader was hospitalized in Tanzania and warned listeners not to pay attention to any contradictory reports on Radio Muhabura, particularly interviews with Kanyarengwe, because to "hear someone does not prevent him from being ill or wounded".[20]

3   Denouncing "Traitors"

Despite the fact that a cease-fire had been in effect since March 1993, one month before RTLM was formally established, the station operated with the siege mentality of the early 1990s. Like *Kangura* and the other pro-MRND newspapers, RTLM frequently denounced opposition figures and government critics as "enemies" or "traitors", accusing them of working for the RPF. Before the genocide, RTLM had mostly targeted high-profile individuals, particularly opposition members of the coalition transitional government, and leaders of civil society, who publicly supported the Arusha Accords. Human rights activists and journalists who filed critical reports of the MRND, the CDR or the "Hutu Power" movement, were also at risk (see Political Background chapter, note 42). CDR or "Hutu Power" leaders, however, were never attacked by RTLM and were frequently studio guests.

Given the strong militia presence and tension in Kigali, it was intimidating even for government officials to be accused of working for the RPF. RTLM broadcasters appear to have been well aware of this fact. In late October 1993, RTLM warned listeners that it intended to continue singling out individuals on the air, regardless of their reaction or protests. One announcer explained:

> RTLM is a private radio! The reason why our radio surprises you is because you were not used to this type of talk on Radio Rwanda. We can understand, that is why you hear people complaining, 'RTLM is talking about me!' It will say even

more. Now we are just making you familiar. We
will keep on increasing, increasing.[21]

In many cases, the same individuals were regularly denounced by
RTLM. Faustin Twagiramungu of the MDR, who had been designated
future Prime Minister under the Arusha Accords, reported to
ARTICLE 19 that the station repeatedly called him an "assassin" and
"traitor", accusing him of having "sold the party to the RPF". Landoald
Ndasingwa, Minister of Labour and Social Affairs in the transitional
government and leader of the PL's moderate tendency, was also
frequently attacked. One of the few Tutsi to hold a cabinet position in
the transitional government, he challenged conventional attitudes
towards ethnicity and was well-known for saying, "I am Tutsi, my
wife is a white Canadian, several members of my family are married
to Hutu, in fact we are all tired of this ethnic business".[22] RTLM
reportedly alleged he was working for the RPF, repeatedly accusing
him of "paving the way for his brothers from Uganda" (a reference to
the RPF). Ndasingwa, who walked with a limp, was also mocked by
the radio for his physical disability.

While government figures were constantly denigrated on RTLM,
many had access to guards and security services provided by the state.
In contrast, journalists and leaders of civil society were clearly more
vulnerable. Nkiko Nsengimana, Co-ordinator of the *Centre Iwacu*, a
research centre which worked on rural development issues, was targeted by RTLM after the *Centre* issued public statements in early 1994
calling for the government to implement the Arusha Accords, which
had been repeatedly delayed. After this campaign, RTLM frequently
reported that *Centre Iwacu* staff were "working for the enemy".

Independent and opposition newspapers were systematically
attacked by RTLM and labelled "newspapers of the enemy". Gaspard
Karemera, Editor of *Imbaga*, a publication affiliated with the *Centre
Iwacu*, reported that he was targeted by both *Kangura* and RTLM
after publishing an article in late February 1994 on the rise of the
"Hutu Power" movement within the MDR party. In March, *Kangura*
published a commentary on Karemera and accused his wife, employed
by UNICEF in Nairobi, of serving the RPF. In late March, RTLM
broadcast the *Kangura* article several times.

RTLM Before the Genocide

Other RTLM broadcasters went beyond denunciations and issued veiled threats, flaunting their impunity. Agathe Uwilingiyimana, of the MDR, who served as Prime Minister from July 1993 until she was killed on 7 April 1994, was threatened and ridiculed. A broadcast on 3 December 1993 warned:

> The Prime Minister has created a bad atmosphere because she co-operates with the RPF. She should remember that the scar she has was previously a wound.[23]

This was a reference to an assault Agathe Uwilingiyimana suffered in 1992 when intruders, allegedly from the MRND, broke into her home and beat her severely. She is reported to have received further death threats, broadcast in February and March 1994, including one which warned that she was "not immortal".

On 3 April 1994, *Rwanda Rushya* journalist Joseph Mudatsikira was threatened by Noël Hitimana on RTLM. In the course of a commentary on an unrelated subject, Hitimana suddenly shouted Mudatsikira's name and continued:

> Let me say Hello, child of my mother. Let me salute you, as you are the same as Noheli [a journalist]. ... If you die just as everyone has been speaking about you, it is not like dying like a sheep, without having been spoken of. When we have spoken about you, you have been effectively spoken of.

In characteristic RTLM style, Hitimana threatened the journalist while pretending to be on familiar terms with him. He then joked about the fact that he was singling out the journalist, as if it were an honour to be mentioned on RTLM. According to Hitimana, this meant that Mudatsikira would not die passively and anonymously, "like a sheep". Joseph Mudatsikira was killed in the genocide which began just a few days later. The circumstances of his death are unknown.

4   Radio for the Militias

In Rwanda, the MRND and CDR party militias were already well-established and active by the time RTLM was created. From its inception, RTLM demonstrated several links to the militias and death squad. A significant number of high-level militia members and "Network Zero" leaders were involved in creating and financially supporting the radio station (See Chapter 4, Section 2). Moreover, a number of individuals were targeted by RTLM because they had tried to criticize or stop militia activities.

General Augustin Ndindiliyimana, the Head of the gendarmerie, reported that, in late 1993, a sergeant manning a roadblock in the town of Nyanza, Butare *préfecture*, was denounced by RTLM. A few hours previously, he had tried to disarm a large group of armed *Interahamwe*, travelling to a MRND meeting in Butare *préfecture*, an area where the party had little support. The militia members resisted and the gendarme failed to disarm the group. Later that day, RTLM announced that the sergeant was an "enemy and RPF agent".

Joseph Matata, the Executive Secretary of the *Association Rwandaise pour la Défense des Droits de l'Homme* (Rwandan human rights organization — ARDHO) reported to ARTICLE 19 that he was subject to regular denunciations by RTLM after publishing a series of reports on violence by the militias. On 26 November 1993, he produced a document on inter-ethnic massacres, which described violations by the *Interahamwe* in Mayange *secteur*, Kanzenze *commune*, in the Bugesera region. Later in the same week, RTLM claimed that Matata was an RPF agent and, from late November onwards, he was denounced approximately once a week by RTLM, which accused him of hating the military and people from the North, where support for the MRND was strongest. On 20 December, ARDHO published a report on an incident in Taba, Gitarama *préfecture*, in which 17 schoolchildren were killed in a grenade attack. According to Matata, Silas Kubwimana, a local businessman and alleged financial supporter of the militias in that area, informed RTLM broadcasters of the report and asked them to denounce the human rights activist.

After receiving threats from the militias and local civil servants where he lived in Gitega *secteur*, Nyarugenge *commune*, in Kibungo *préfecture*, Joseph Matata fled to Kigali, where he stayed for several months, continuing to campaign against militia activity. On 12 Feburary 1994, he delivered a letter addressed to the Head of the Kibungo gendarmerie in Rwamagana, warning that there could be militia violence following a scheduled MRND meeting in the town the next day. ARDHO called for the gendarmes to intervene to protect the local communities from possible pillage. According to Matata, the letter did not reach the Commandant but instead was redirected to MRND leaders in the area, who read it aloud at a party meeting the following morning. That afternoon, RTLM announcers broadcast excerpts of the letter. They also denounced Matata as an "enemy of the MRND youth group" and claimed that his reports on human rights abuses were "at the root of the turmoil in this region".

By virtue of RTLM's *de facto* relationship to the militias and death squads, individuals who were denounced or even cited by its broadcasters risked attacks by these clandestine organizations. Journalist Sixbert Musangamfura explained:

> I listened to it [RTLM] constantly because every time RTLM alluded to someone, you were sure to see the *Interahamwe* head out shortly afterwards. Also, people who were prudent absolutely needed to listen to this station in case they were mentioned. [If this happened] you knew you had to change your address that day.[24]

Most of the Rwandan journalists and human rights activists interviewed by ARTICLE 19 indicated that they tried to take precautions for their personal security if they were named by RTLM. In some cases, people tried to convince the station's broadcasters to change or correct what had been said about them. On 24 December 1993, BBC Swahili Service stringer Ali Yusuf Mugenzi was accused by Kantano Habimana of having reported that RTLM belonged to the CDR party. Mugenzi had filed a report for the BBC which noted that RTLM was principally owned by CDR supporters. Habimana warned: "Tell him [Mugenzi] to come here. This is not a CDR station". According to Mugenzi, "such a statement could be like a death warrant in Rwanda". He repeatedly telephoned the radio station that day and pleaded with its broadcasters to change what they had said about him, explaining that he feared he would be attacked as a result. Two days later RTLM finally retracted the statement.

In addition to naming and threatening particular individuals, RTLM broadcast warnings directly from the militia leaders themselves. On 3 April 1994, RTLM relayed a message from the "Zulus", a division of the *Interahamwe*:

> The Zulus are issuing a warning to a group of people who live in the Nyakabanda zone ... of Remera in the SGP, who are walking around with the *Inkotanyi* under the pretext that they are their relatives.[25]

Noël Hitimana alleged that the previous night a group of "*Inkotanyi*" had attacked the "Zulus" in the Kigali neighbourhood of Remera and had attempted to assassinate their "President", Aloys Ngirabatware, but were repelled by other members of the *Interahamwe*. The "Zulus" had apparently asked RTLM to broadcast a warning to the people in that neighbourhood.

The alleged attack on Ngirabatware was a pretext or token justification for this warning. RTLM did not explicitly state what was threatened nor the precise group of people who were the intended recipients of this message. Although RTLM did not directly accuse the RPA of involvement in the supposed attack, it insinuated that the alleged perpetrators were allies of the rebels.

Hitimana went on to identify another group targeted by the "Zulus". In this second case, the threat of violence was explicit:

> They [the "Zulus"] say 'we are issuing a final warning. ... to the drivers who run the "taxi" service who have gone to pick up the *Inkotanyi* at the CND'. They [the Zulus] say 'we warn you, those who drive the taxis' ... if they [the Zulus] rip them [the drivers] into little pieces, they should not claim that they had not been warned. ... Musabyimana Emile, then, do you hear all that? Kiloso, do you hear that? Karisa, do you hear that? Kwetu, you

> hear that? ... They should not say that we haven't
> warned them.

The pretext for targeting taxi drivers was the allegation that they accepted RPF soldiers as customers. The CND was the parliament building where a battalion of 600 RPA soldiers was stationed. The reference to the violence which the militia threatened was chillingly direct. At the end of the announcement, Hitimana accredited the message to the "Head of the Disciplinary Section" of the "Zulus", Paul Zikanga.

There were instances when militia members responded to ambiguous calls for action made by RTLM. Early in the morning of 24 or 25 February 1994, RTLM announced that the RPF battalion stationed at the CND had begun an offensive and was infiltrating the local population in Kigali. The station called on people to "search" for RPA troops in their neighbourhoods, particularly in Kimisaga. Witnesses reported to ARTICLE 19 that militias erected roadblocks in this neighbourhood almost immediately after the broadcast and began harassing local people. Later that day, militia members conducted raids in Kimisaga, broke into several houses, and threatened the Tutsi living there. Françoise Kagoyire, wife of *Imbaga* journalist Gratien Karambizi,[26] and dozens of other people, were forced to flee the area. UNAMIR troops are reported to have intervened that evening to stop the violence and the residents were able to return the following morning.

5   RTLM Broadcasts: A Breach of Law and Contract

In its broadcasts from October 1993 onwards, RTLM frequently violated both the terms of its contract and the 1991 Press Law which includes several articles governing broadcasting. According to the *"Convention d'Etablissement et d'Exploitation de Radiodiffusion ou de Télévision"* ("Convention on the Establishment and Operation of Radio and Television") between the government and RTLM, signed by Minister of Information, Faustin Rucogoza, and President of the

RTLM Board of Directors, Félicien Kabuga, RTLM specifically undertook to refrain from engaging in hate speech or incitement to violence. Article 5(2) states: "RTLM undertakes ... not to broadcast programmes likely to incite hatred, violence or any form of division".[27] In addition, Article 5(1) maintains that RTLM must respect the right of reply and Article 5(7) states that the station will adhere to basic principles of journalistic ethics.

RTLM also clearly violated the 1991 Press Law on several accounts, including Article 27, which guarantees the right of reply. Moreover, the hate speech and inflammatory commentaries following the assassination of Burundian President Ndadaye were in violation of Article 46 of the Press Law and Article 166 of the 1977 Penal Code. The draconian Article 166 of the Penal Code states that it is a crime, punishable by 2-10 years in prison and a fine of between Rwfr2,000 and Rwfr100,000 (between US$12 and US$595) to "incite the population to revolt against the established authorities, either to incite or attempt to incite conflict amongst the population or to cause alarm and seek to bring turmoil to the territory of the Republic".[28]

RTLM received several formal warnings from Minister of Information, Faustin Rucogoza, and Director of ORINFOR, Jean-Marie Vianney Higiro, about these breaches of law and contract. In a letter of 25 October 1993, addressed to RTLM's Directors, the Minister of Information noted:

> [RTLM] has used the *putsch* carried out by the Burundian army against the democratically elected government as a pretext to broadcast communiqués and programmes which can incite violence and undermine the path towards unity and national reconciliation advocated by the Arusha Accords.[29]

On 26 November 1993, Minister Rucogoza summoned Félicien Kabuga to his office and warned him again about the "divisive" broadcasts of RTLM.[30] In a second meeting with RTLM managers on 10 February 1994, Rucogoza stated that the station was continuing to spread "rumours likely to provoke conflict within the country". In addition, he expressed concern about the anti-Tutsi propaganda on RTLM:

> RTLM has a tendency to liken all the members of
> the RPF to the Tutsi; to liken the domestic political
> opposition to the RPF; to reduce political problems
> in Rwanda to ethnic hatred between Hutu and Tutsi;
> to liken the Tutsi from the country to the *Inkotanyi*;
> and to make the population believe that all the
> problems of the country emanate from the Tutsi.[31]

In March 1994, the Director of ORINFOR wrote a letter to the RTLM Directors in which he underlined the concerns raised by the Minister of Information.

Although Minister Rucogoza does not appear to have taken any punitive measures against RTLM, several members of the government initiated civil defamation cases against individual broadcasters. These cases were blocked by the *Tribunal de la première instance* (Tribunal of First Instance). Former Public Prosecutor Alphonse-Marie Nkubito reported to ARTICLE 19 that he was discouraged by President Habyarimana from taking any steps to prosecute RTLM journalists.

In addition to formal complaints by Rwandan officials, members of the international diplomatic community informally expressed concern about RTLM in meetings with President Habyarimana. They appear to have criticized the station for undermining the Arusha Accords rather than for inciting ethnic hatred and violence, in violation of Rwandan law. According to the Joint Evaluation of Emergency Assistance to Rwanda:

> Unable to agree among themselves on the signifi-
> cance of the radio [station] and how to silence it,
> the donors limited themselves to making yet
> another representation to Habyarimana. The latter
> responded as usual by promising to look into it,
> and there the matter rested.[32]

The possibility of jamming RTLM was apparently discussed at the US Department of Defence at this stage (See Chapter 6, section 10), but not seriously considered.[33] On 3 April 1994, the German Ambassador, speaking on behalf of the European Union (EU), whose Presidency Germany then held, appears to have been referring to RTLM when he stated that the EU "wishes to point out the unacceptable role of some media which are blocking the indispensable climate of national reconciliation".[34]

6   3 April 1994: Announcing the Apocalypse

In the months leading up to the genocide, several government-sponsored "hate" media made various "predictions" which suggested they were aware that widespread massacres were being prepared. Extremist media warned that there would be a bloodbath in Rwanda, while trying to conceal that the violence would be orchestrated by their own camp, hardliners in the military and the MRND militia. Instead, RTLM and *Kangura* claimed that the RPF was planning to launch an attack which would trigger widespread violence throughout the country. *Kangura* published several reports to this effect. One article, in January 1994, headlined "Who Will Survive the War of March?", claimed that the RPF had acquired reinforcements and that troops at the CND already numbered 3,000, instead of the 600 agreed upon during the peace negotiations.[35] The article ominously concluded: "If the RPF have [*sic*] decided to kill us ... then let us kill each other. Let whatever is smouldering erupt".[36]

In February, *Kangura* declared that the battle with the RPF would be massive. An article headlined, "The Final Attack" warned, "We have indications that the RPF will soon launch other attacks in Kigali from all sides".[37] *Kangura* then used the predicted RPF hostilities as a pretext to threaten the rebels, referring to them abusively as "*Inyenzi*", a term understood to mean Tutsi generally. It continued: "We know where the cockroaches are. If they look for us, they had better watch out".[38] Another government-sponsored "hate" newspaper, *La Médaille Nyiramacibiri*, suggested that Tutsi civilians could be eliminated in the course of this attack in February 1994, it published an article headlined, "By the way, the Tutsi race could be extinguished".[39] *Kangura* also predicted that the President would be killed by the RPF within a few weeks. Its Editor, Hassan Ngeze, wrote:

> ... Last month we saw undeniable signs showing
> how Habyarimana is going to be killed. ... shot dead
> by a person taken from the Rwandan Armed Forces.
> ... That person will be a Hutu bought by *Inyenzi*.[40]

Although the press close to the CDR and the MRND made obscure allusions to the violence which was to overtake the country, on 3 April 1994, three days before the genocide, RTLM provided a more specific and graphic description of what was about to happen. Like the previous warnings in the press, RTLM claimed that the RPF was planning to violate the cease-fire and to overthrow the Rwandan government: "The RPF rebels want to take power. Take it by the use of arms. They want to do 'a little something'". The RTLM broadcaster claimed that his informants inside the RPF had confirmed the dates of the planned invasion:

> They have dates, we know them. ... we have agents
> ... who bring us the information. They tell us this:
> on the 3rd, the 4th, and the 5th, there will be a little
> something here in Kigali City. And also on the 7th
> and the 8th ... you will hear the sound of bullets or
> grenades explode. ... But I hope that the Rwandan
> armed forces are on the alert.[41]

Wednesday 6 April 1994, the date of the plane crash which killed President Habyarimana and marked the beginning of the genocide, is conspicuously omitted from this prediction of what was about to take place. The second time the broadcaster mentioned the dates he noted that the RPF would "rest on the 6th", before resuming the following day. RTLM implied that its information was something of an inside joke, and failed to state specifically what would occur; the station repeatedly referred to the forthcoming unnamed event as "a little something". The only clue provided was that it would be mounted with "bullets and grenades".

According to RTLM, the "little something" was to be used as a mere distraction or camouflage for something bigger which was to follow, the *"Simusiga"*[42] or "final attack:

> But in fact, they are planning the *"Simusiga"* ...
> they say that when we have finished this little some-
> thing ... disrupting the city, we will turn to the
> *"Simusiga"* ... but as to the date itself, my agent
> has not yet told me ...[43]

Not an end in itself, the "little something" would serve as a decoy, to draw public attention elsewhere. The larger attack would then follow and take the country by surprise. The broadcaster declared himself unable or unwilling to provide any information about the *"Simusiga"*, claiming his informant had not yet given him the dates. In retrospect, the "little something" may have been a reference to plans to shoot down the Presidential aeroplane, and the *"Simusiga"*, a soubriquet for the genocide, which was to immediately follow. The *"Simusiga"* or "Final Battle" was how RTLM would refer to the genocide as it occurred over the next three and a half months.

RTLM went on to claim that some Tutsi, "moderate Tutsi ... who are humble", were against these alleged RPF plans to invade and tried to warn the rebels not to go ahead with this move which would lead to widespread killings. The broadcaster began to detail the bloodshed which was about to occur. According to RTLM, "moderate Tutsi" had complained to the RPF about "these things ... involving disturbances, spilling yet more blood, whereas we are satiated". The broadcaster indicated that civilians were about to be killed and warned: "The RPF soldiers need to understand ... that they will not benefit from killing their Hutu relatives, killing their Tutsi relatives". After portraying FPR rebels as bloodthirsty and indifferent to the deaths of their own "relatives", he suddenly launched into a description of the enormity of the bloodshed which was expected. Beginning solemnly in French and then continuing in Kinyarwanda, RTLM's broadcaster warned:

> Let the RPF realize that it will answer to the
> People and to History for the youth it has
> continued to decimate [said solemnly in French].
> Let the RPF listen up: in the face of world history,
> in history and to the People. ... One day it ... [the
> RPF] will have to explain to the People and to all
> of Humanity ... how these children of the country,

these children of the country, they [the RPF]
hastened them to death ... One day they [the RPF]
will explain.[44]

Still blaming the RPF for the genocide which would be orchestrated
by the security forces and militias, RTLM warned that the magnitude
of the bloodshed would be great.

After indicating the gravity of what was to happen, the broadcaster changed his tone and joked about the bloodbath which he
expected. Mocking RPF leader Tito Rutaremara and imitating his voice,
he continued:

Ha! Rutaremara, if you are listening, you will tell
...them [beginning soberly and later changing tone]
'Hey, yo yo yo so what? That's how it is in times of
war'. ... ha. Yeeee!!!!! Yes, you will say it like this:
'It is like that in times of war, shyeu. ...Yeee Ha
Ha. You cannot pick up spilled blood.[45] Blood can
be spilled but it cannot be picked up. Ha heeee [said
in a menacing tone]. ... We will have news about
all of that.[46]

He alleged that the rebel leader would revel in bloodshed and show no
remorse, gleefully alluding to the gory details of the coming genocide.

This broadcast ended with a specific warning to President Juvénal
Habyarimana, threatening that Rwandans would not tolerate a Head
of State who no longer had popular support. The announcer concluded:

But in fact ... the people, they are the true shield.
They are the real army, which is strong ... the armed
forces fight but the people hold the rear, we are the
shield. The day when the people stand up and no
longer want you and when they hate you ... from
the bottom of their hearts, when you make them
nauseous ... I wonder how you will escape? How
can you get out? You cannot govern someone who
does not want you. That is impossible. And even
Habyarimana himself, if the citizens no longer

> wanted him, he would no longer be able to enter
> his office. It is impossible.[47]

Maintaining that RTLM was the station of the "majority", the broadcaster claimed to know the wishes and beliefs of "the people" in Rwanda who, he suggested, could be driven to use force to oust their opponents, comparing the population to the FAR. RTLM claimed that anyone who upset the masses should be prepared to face death at their hands. The broadcaster ended by warning that there would be no escape.

Notes

[1] As quoted in, Joint Evaluation of Emergency Assistance to Rwanda, *The International Response to Conflict and Genocide: Lessons from the Rwanda Experience, (Study 2: Early Warning and Conflict Management),* (Denmark: Steering Committee of the Joint Evaluation of Emergency Assistance to Rwanda, March 1996), 86.

[2] Lindsey Hilsum, "The Radio Station Whose Call Sign is Mass Murder", *The Observer*, 15 May 1994.

[3] For example, Jean-Pierre Chrétien writes, "La puissante influence de 'radio-la-haine' ne peut pourtant s'expliquer sans faire référence à son caractère professionnel". ("The powerful influence of the 'hate radio' cannot be explained without reference to its professional quality".) J-P Chrétien, *Rwanda: Les médias du génocide* (Paris: Éditions Karthala, 1995), 71.

[4] "Mal informés" because the "médias officiels ont ... gardé leur 'langue de bois' traditionnelle'". G Gahigi, "Impact des médias privés et opinion publique rwandaise", in *Dialogue* (April-May 1994), 15-19.

[5] "Il y a quelqu'un qui vient de me téléphoner et il a dit: 'Noheli comment se fait-il que tu es si euphorique, qu'est-ce qui s'est passé? hein? Je soupçonne que tu es venu après avoir 'exorcisé le mauvais sort' mon vieux!' Ha! ... Et moi je lui ai répondu qu'il s'agit seulement de boire du thé, enfant de ma mère, sauf que le sucre est devenu introuvable".
Hitimana used a traditional expression to broach the taboo subject of alcoholism and joke about the extent of his drinking. To "exorcise the evil spirit" is an expression referring to an old Rwandan belief that one is guaranteed good luck for the day if one drinks or eats something just before leaving one's home in the morning. Hitimana admitted to drinking alcohol early in

the day but did so humorously, saying "it is just a matter of drinking tea". This is a well-known Rwandan joke referring to one who tries to hide the fact that he is consuming alcohol by drinking it in a tea cup. The phrase, "child of my mother" is an expression of great familiarity and affection. (Unless otherwise indicated, RTLM transcripts were gathered and translated from Kinyarwanda by ARTICLE 19.)

[6] A slang expression implying that if one is going to do something mischievous, one may as well go all the way. Its English equivalent would be "One may as well be hanged for a sheep as a lamb".

[7] RTLM, 17-31 Oct. 1993, translated from Kinyarwanda to English, Human Rights Watch (unpublished Human Rights Watch transcript).

[8] G Prunier, *The Rwanda Crisis 1959-1994: History of a Genocide* (London and New York: Hurst & Company and Columbia University Press, 1995), 199.

[9] RTLM, note 7 above.

[10] Ibid.

[11] *Ijambo*, no. 61, quoted by RTLM, note 7 above.

[12] Ibid.

[13] Ibid.

[14] Ibid.

[15] RTLM, note 7 above.

[16] Ibid.

[17] Ibid.

[18] Ibid.

[19] Ibid.

[20] Ibid.

[21] Ibid.

[22] As quoted in Prunier, note 8 above, at 125.

[23] As cited in C Mironko and S Cook, "Broadcasting racism, reaping genocide: Radio Television Libre des Milles Collines (RTLM) and the Rwandan genocide", paper presented at the Annual Conference of the American Anthropological Association, Washington, 16 Nov. 1995.

[24] "Je l'écoutais à tout moment car chaque fois que la RTLM désignait

quelqu'un, vous étiez sûrs de voir débarquer peu après les *Interahamwe*. Aussi, les gens prudents devaient absolument écouter cette radio au cas où ils seraient cités. Vous saviez que vous devriez changer d'adresse le même jour". Reporters sans frontières, *Rwanda: médias de la haine ou presse démocratique? Rapport de mission 16-24 Sept. 1994* (Paris: RSF, 1994).

[25] "Les Zulus mettent donc en garde un groupe de gens, qui vivent dans la zone de Nyakabanda ... de Remera au SGP, qui se baladent avec des *Inkotanyi* sous prétexte qu'ils ont avec eux des liens de parenté".

[26] Gratien Karambizi was later killed during the genocide.

[27] "La RTLM s'engage à ... [n]e pas diffuser les émissions de nature à inciter à la haine, à la violence et à toute forme de division". *Convention d'Etablissment et d'Exploitation de Radiodiffusion ou de Télévision*, in Reporters sans frontières, note 24 above.

[28] *18 août 1977 – Décret-loi no. 21/77, Des infractions et de leur répression en particulier, Section II: Des atteintes à la sûreté de l'Etat (Code penal Rwandais, Livre II), J.O., 1978, n.1., 259.*

[29] "a pris prétexte du putsch perpétré par l'armée burundaise contre le gouvernement démocratiquement élu ... pour diffuser des communiqués et [des] émissions qui peuvent inciter à la violence et saper la voie de l'unité et de la réconciliation nationale prônée par les accords d'Arusha". Reporters sans frontières, *Rwanda: l'impasse. La liberté de la presse après le génocide 4 juillet 1994–28 août 1995* (Paris: Sept. 1995), 32.

[30] Ibid.

[31] "RTLM a tendance à assimiler tous les membres du FPR aux Tutsi, à assimiler l'opposition politique de l'intérieur au FPR, à réduire les problèmes politiques du Rwanda à la haine ethnique entre Hutu et Tutsi, à assimiler les Tutsi de l'intérieur aux *Inkotanyi* et à faire comprendre à la population que (tous) les maux dont souffre le pays (viennent des) Tutsi". Ibid.

[32] Joint Evaluation of Emergency Assistance to Rwanda, *The International Response to Conflict and Genocide: Lessons from the Rwanda Experience, (Study 2: Early Warning and Conflict Management)*, (Denmark: Steering Committee of the Joint Evaluation of Emergency Assistance to Rwanda, March 1996), 86.

[33] Ibid., at 87.

[34] Radio Rwanda, *BBC Summary of World Broadcasts*, 3 April 1994.

[35] *Kangura*, no. 55, Jan. 1994.

[36] As cited in African Rights, *Death, Despair and Defiance*, Revised Edition (London: African Rights, 1995), 73.

[37] *Kangura* no. 57, Feb. 1994, 4, as cited in, Reporters sans frontières, note 24 above.

[38] "Là où sont maintenant les cafards, on le sait. S'ils nous cherchent, qu'ils fassent attention". Ibid.

[39] Prunier, note 8 above, at 222.

[40] As cited in African Rights, note 36 above, at 73.

[41] "Ils ont des dates, nous les connaissons. Nous connaissons ces dates aussi. ... nous avons des agents, yeah! Oh ho ho! Il y a là nos agents, il y a des agents qui nous font parvenir les informations. Ils nous disent ainsi: à la date du 3, du 4, du 5, hm, ils disent qu'il doit y avoir une petite chose, ici à Kigali, Kigali-ville. Et même à la date du 7 et du 8, hm. Et alors vous entendrez le bruit des balles ou encore vous entendrez les grenades tonner. ... A la date du 3, du 4, et du 5, il est attendu qu'une petite chose va survenir ici à Kigali, et même ils vont poursuivre et se reposer à la date du 6, et à la date du 7 et du 8, ils vont faire une petite chose, en utilisant ces balles et grenades. Mais j'espère que les forces armées rwandaises sont en éveil".

[42] Its literal meaning, "I will no longer spare him", translates as "the final attack".

[43] "Mais en réalité, il y a l'attaque *Simusiga* qu'ils prévoient, et ils disent quand nous aurons fini cette petite chose de perturber la ville, nous allons nous y mettre avec l'attaque *Simusiga* après cela, mais quand à la date elle-même, mon agent [du FPR] ne me l'a pas encore dite, il ne me l'a pas encore dite".

[44] "Que le FPR sache qu'il répondra devant le Peuple et l'Histoire, de cette jeunesse qu'il ne cesse de faire décimer [*dit en français et d'un ton très solonnel*]. Que le FPR entende bien: devant l'Histoire du monde, devant l'Histoire et devant le Peuple. ... Un jour, il devra expliquer devant le Peuple et l'Humanité entière ... comment ces enfants du pays, ces enfants du pays, ils les ont précipité dans la Mort...ils les ont précipité dans la Mort. ... Un jour ils l'expliqueront. ..."

[45] Rwandan proverb which means one should not die without reason.

[46] "Ha! Rutaremara [Tito Rutaremara, haut cadre et député FPR] si tu m'écoutes, tu leur di...tu leur diras [parodiant comiquement le rire et la voix de Rutaremara]: "Heu, yo yo yo yo et alors? C'est ainsi en temps de guerre" ... ha. Yeeee!!!!, Oui, tu le diras comme ça: "C'est comme ça avec la guerre,

shyeu. ... Yeee Ha Ha. ... Le sang se verse mais ne se ramasse pas [proverbe rwandais]. Le sang se verse il ne se ramasse pas, Ha heeeein [exclamation insistante de menace et d'avertissement]. ... On en aura des nouvelles de tout ça. ..."

[47] "Mais en fait ... le peuple, voilà le vrai bouclier, c'est la véritable armée qui est forte... les forces armées combattent mais le peuple lui il dit: nous tenons vos arrières, c'est nous le bouclier. Le jour où le peuple va se lever et qu'il ne voudra plus de vous, qu'il vous haïra ... du fond de son coeur, quand vous lui inspirez la nausée, je ... je me demande par où vous vous échapperez. Par où pouvez-vous passer? Tu ne peux gouverner celui qui ne veut pas de toi. Cela est impossible. Et même Habyarimana lui-même, si les citoyens n'en voulaient plus, il ne pourrait plus entrer dans son bureau. C'est impossible".

Chapter 6

RTLM AND THE GENOCIDE

R TLM appears to have reached its peak of activity during the genocide, reportedly broadcasting 24 hours a day throughout the first
several weeks of the genocide and then daily with a more limited
schedule for the rest of the three and a half month period. RTLM
welcomed the self-proclaimed interim government upon its formation
on 8 April 1994 and never acknowledged that it had effectively come
to power through a *coup d'état*. Nor did the radio station ever reveal
the atrocities which the interim government and its security forces
were committing. Glossing over the fact that most of the opposition
cabinet members of the transitional coalition government had been
killed, or forced into hiding by the evening of 8 April, broadcasters
Valérie Bemeriki and Noël Hitimana reassured listeners of the new
government's legality.

Meanwhile, as independent journalists were hunted down and
killed during the early weeks of the genocide, RTLM journalists
received special protection from the interim authorities. Foreign
correspondents covering the genocide reported that the authorities
prevented them from visiting RTLM's premises. Unless authorized by
the Minister of Defence, they could neither meet nor interview RTLM
broadcasters.[1] Mark Doyle, from the BBC, noted that the Belgian RTLM
journalist, Georges Ruggiu, had free access to the heavily guarded Hôtel
des Diplomates, which housed high-level interim government officials,
where access was strictly off-limits to anyone else.

1 The Plane Crash and the Proclamation of the New Government

Having predicted, just a few days earlier, that a "little something" would
soon happen, RTLM was the first source to announce the plane crash
which killed President Juvénal Habyarimana around 8.30 p.m. on the
evening of 6 April 1994. The station reportedly broadcast information

about the downing of the plane by 9.00 p.m., within an hour of the crash; Radio Burundi, Radio France Internationale and other international radio stations reported the news later that night. Neither Radio Rwanda nor the armed forces made any statement about the President's death until the following day.[2] President Habyarimana and the President of Burundi, Cyprien Ntaryamira, had been returning from a meeting of regional Heads of State in Tanzania, where President Habyarimana had been pressured to cease obstructing and immediately implement the Arusha Accords. No investigation into the crash has been conclusive, however, it is widely believed that the aircraft was shot down by extremists who vehemently opposed and tried to block the implementation of the Arusha Accords.[3] The official explanation advanced by both the interim government and RTLM over the following few days was that the plane had been shot down by the RPF, assisted by the Belgian contingent of UNAMIR.

RTLM was also the first station to broadcast news of the inauguration of the self-proclaimed interim government on 8 April. Claiming to be a coalition government, in fact, all "opposition" representatives were members of the extremist "Hutu Power" factions of parties close to the MRND (see Political Background chapter, page 19). As Bemeriki and Hitimana announced the new cabinet, they joked of how opposition representatives of the transitional government, who had been assassinated or had gone into hiding, were being replaced because they could no longer be found. Bemeriki began:

> ... Nzamurambaho [former Minister of Agriculture] ... we don't know what has happened to him ... the Ministry of Primary and Secondary Education ... will be headed by Monsieur Rwamakuba André. .. I don't know where Jean-Marie Vianney [Mbonimpa] could be, him either ... I really don't know how that happened. ... [Bemeriki tries to hold back from laughing and Hitimana begins to giggle]. We don't know much, but maybe ... we will find out. ... but now we don't know. ... Thus, we don't know about Lando [Landoald Ndasingwa], as for him ... maybe "they" [the opposition members of Cabinet] have resigned ... .[4]

By the time of the broadcast, Minister of Primary and Secondary Education, Jean-Marie Vianney Mbonimpa, had fled. Frédéric Nzamurambaho, President of the PSD and Minister of Agriculture and Livestock, was reportedly taken from his home by Presidential Guards during the day of 7 April and executed. Landoald Ndasingwa, PL leader, and Minister of Labour and Social Affairs, was also killed the same day, along with his Canadian wife, their two children and his mother.

By mentioning people who had just been assassinated, the announcers suggested that they had inside knowledge of the executions which were in process. Far from denouncing the killings or expressing concern at the whereabouts of these figures, Bemeriki professed ignorance about their cases. She insisted that their disappearances were all random occurrences and claimed that the Ministers must have simply wandered off. As her colleague, Hitimana, began to laugh, she repeated: "We don't know know much ... We don't know much". Leaving listeners in suspense as to the dreadful fate of their leaders, Bemeriki added that she expected to soon find out what had happened to them: "but maybe ... we will find out. ... but now we don't know".

Further into the broadcast, Bemeriki and Hitimana began relaying some of the morbid news. After criticizing Prime Minister Agathe Uwilingiyimana at some length, Hitimana suddenly interrupted Bemeriki, exclaiming with mock surprise: "People have said that she has answered the call of God [that she is dead] ... as for myself, this is the first that I learn of it". Agathe Uwilingiyimana had been killed in the early morning of 7 April, after leaving her home, which was guarded by several UNAMIR troops, to join her husband, hiding in the house of a Senegalese neighbour. Her UNAMIR escort was ordered by its UN High Command not to follow her and to withdraw protection. Rwandan security forces tracked down the couple a few hours later and executed them on the spot. Ten Belgian UNAMIR troops guarding Uwilingiyimana's home were then disarmed by Rwandan security forces, taken to a military camp, and executed.[5]

2   Genocide as "The Final Battle"

> In a final war such as this, there can be no clem-
> ency for people who joke around, be they mem-
> bers of the military or civilians. ... This war is really
> final. ... We must wage a war without mercy.[6]

Despite allegations by the international media, RTLM does not appear
to have explicitly called for people to exterminate Tutsi civilians. The
phrase, "the grave is only half full, who will help us to fill it?" is
frequently accredited to RTLM by the international media, but
ARTICLE 19 has found no evidence in either transcripts or in witness
testimony to support its usage. However, RTLM indirectly, and
systematically, advocated the killings of Tutsi by identifying them with
the RPF who, it claimed, had just invaded Rwanda, assassinated the
President, and would exterminate all the Hutu if the supposed attack
was not immediately repulsed. RTLM described the genocide as a
"final war" or "final battle", claiming the only way to stop the RPF
was to exterminate all the rebels and their alleged "accomplices",
implying all Tutsi civilians in Rwanda.

During the genocide RTLM to a large degree played on extant
fears about the RPF, which had been exacerbated by government
propaganda throughout the years of war from 1990 to 1993. RTLM
echoed this earlier government misinformation with its claims of
systematic and unspeakable atrocities by the rebel group. The images
it portrayed were more graphic than those broadcast earlier by Radio
Rwanda. RTLM warned of "the *Inyenzi*'s thirst for blood", and
alleged:

> ... they [RPF troops] cruelly kill mankind ... they
> kill by dissecting ... by extracting various organs
> from the body ... for example, by taking the heart,
> the liver, the stomach. ... the *inyenzi-inkotanyi* eat
> men.[7]

According to RTLM, this was not a war like any other but a final
confrontation with bloodthirsty monsters, who killed for the sake of
killing. This assertion was underlined by the allegation that the rebels

took pleasure in totally dismembering their victims. Although in the early 1990s, Radio Rwanda had occasionally broadcast reports claiming that the RPF had killed all the civilians in the areas it invaded, it had never portrayed the rebels as likely to annihilate a large section of Rwanda's population. The rebel threat had been presented as ferocious, but limited in scope. During the genocide, however, the RPF was described as evil incarnate, a direct menace to the entire Rwandan population, and to all of humanity.

RTLM claimed that there was no point in negotiating with such a rebel force nor even in fighting it through conventional warfare. According to the station, nothing could rid the rebels of their impulse to kill, and nothing less than their elimination could neutralize the threat they presented. On 3 June 1994, RTLM used this reasoning to try to justify genocide: "... understand that the cruelty of the *Inyenzi* is incurable, the cruelty of the *Inyenzi* can only be cured by their total extermination".[8]

At other times, RTLM described the genocide as punishment which the RPF, and thus the Tutsi, had brought upon themselves through the recent military offensive of 7 April. This alleged attack on the "Hutu majority" by the "Tutsi minority" amounted to "suicide" because the Tutsi had no chance of winning. Openly linking the RPF to the Tutsi generally, Kantano Habimana speculated that the Tutsi were in the process of forging their own destruction, referring to them as "the family which is on its way to extinction in Rwanda".[9] Claiming that the percentage of Tutsi in the Rwandan population had already been reduced from 10 per cent to 8 per cent, he asked, "these people; are they going to continue to commit suicide ... to engage in a suicidal battle against a large group [implying the Hutu or the 'majority'] ... won't they certainly be exterminated?[10] According to this reasoning, the RPF and the Tutsi were not only responsible for the genocide, they could choose to halt it at any point.

RTLM also attempted to justify mass executions of "accomplices", Tutsi who were not members of the RPF, by claiming that this was exactly what the rebels had planned for the Hutu. According to the station, the Hutu would surely have perished had they not defended themselves by attacking first. On 23 May 1994, Habimana claimed that the communal graves in which Tutsi were buried had, in fact, been dug by RPA troops for their intended Hutu victims:

> Kagame had not foreseen that the accomplices, men
> and women, would disappear as a result of the
> action of these citizens, in Kigali, that the graves
> which had been dug for the Hutu were used for the
> accomplices.[11]

In other instances, RTLM described the killing of Tutsi civilians as an
unfortunate but inevitable by-product of the RPF offensive. On 12
June, Habimana accused the RPF of direct responsibility for the
killing of these innocent bystanders:

> these Tutsi have caused the extermination of their
> fellows ... their innocent fellows ... because of an-
> ger ... following the attacks of the *Inkotanyi,* which
> were unjustified.[12]

3   Incitement to Genocide

> If you do not want to have Rwandans exterminated,
> stand up, take action ... without worrying about
> international opinion.[13]

> *Radio-Télévision Libre des Mille Collines, 15 April 1994*

According to RTLM, the "final war" could not be won on the strength
of the Rwandan armed forces alone. It required the participation of the
entire Rwandan population, men and women alike. Along with the
military and administrative authorities, RTLM became an important
vehicle for promoting this "duty" of genocide.

During the genocide, people throughout the country were
compelled, under penalty of death, to co-operate with the security
forces. In many areas, all physically able residents were expected to
man the roadblocks, where individuals had to produce their national
identity cards in order to pass. Instructions were given that those
identified as "Tutsi", and anyone unable to produce an identity card,
were to be executed on the spot. To be found "hiding" at home would

raise suspicion and leave one vulnerable to the roving militias and security forces conducting house-to-house raids in search of the "enemy".

In practice, the situation on the ground was far more complex and many people resisted these instructions in whatever ways they could. ARTICLE 19 received several accounts of how groups organized at the neighbourhood level to try to protect Tutsi and opposition supporters in their areas. There are numerous reports of how people manning roadblocks quietly refused to carry out the orders to kill and instead used their positions at the barriers to assist those trying to escape. *Imbaga* journalist Jean-Baptiste Nkuriyingoma, who later briefly served as Minister of Information under the RPF,[14] was hidden for three months by a neighbour who was in charge of what Nkuriyingoma described as a "good roadblock" in his neighbourhood of Nyamirambo, Kigali. Nkuriyingoma explained: "During the genocide, there were both good and bad roadblocks. The good roadblocks helped people to escape, warned them about spots further up the road where militias were likely to attack". In some cases, people were advised that it would be safer to return to their home areas.

For RTLM, however, no such resistance could be tolerated. On 10 April, the station ordered its listeners to participate in the manhunt:

> Citizens are asked to remain vigilant, to stand up like real men, to defend themselves. The roadblocks must be maintained. They really must be maintained during the day so that that they can halt these *Inkotanyi*. Because there are some [*Inkotanyi*] coming ... dressed as civilians and unarmed ... apparently seeking reinforcements. But citizens really need to stay at their roadblocks, they really must defend themselves, they must remain invincible.[15]

This passage demonstrates the extent to which people were expected to take part in the genocide. It also clearly shows how RTLM had overtly become an arm of government policy. Stating that all the Tutsi targeted were RPF agents and denying that it was demanding that people kill civilians, RTLM claimed that all the Tutsi fleeing for their lives, without any visible signs of RPF involvement, "dressed as civilians and unarmed", were, somehow, travelling to procure military reinforcements. According to RTLM, citizens who killed proved themselves to be "real men", and saved their country from total destruction.

Repeating what amounted to a clear call for violence, RTLM insisted that people at the barriers must fight these RPF agents with all their might:

> Let them [the citizens] stay and fight them [the RPF]
> and really demolish them ... you really need to stand
> firm, you must fight these enemies, really ravage
> them, in short, defend yourselves.[16]

The language RTLM used to incite genocide indicated that the aim of this "battle" was not simply to win the armed combat but rather to utterly destroy the opponent. Occasionally the analogy of the battle-field was dropped in favour of something more direct. On 13 April, Habimana told listeners: "continue to keep your eyes open, remain vigilant ... and give them the punishment they deserve".

The station also issued more specific instructions as to what measures people manning the roadblocks were expected to take. In May 1994, RTLM broadcast an order from a member of the CDR militia, the *Impuzamugambi*, who warned:

> Whoever does not have his identity card should be
> arrested and maybe lose his head there. ... check-
> ing is necessary, one should have his identity card
> with him, showing that he is Rwandan and that he
> is a son of [a] cultivator[17], that he is not an enemy
> or an accomplice, that he is not an *Inkotanyi*.[18]

RTLM did not merely issue stern instructions to kill, it acted as the drumbeat behind the violence, goading and cheering the perpetrators of genocide. On 13 April, one week after the genocide had begun, already claiming the lives of the major opposition figures and approximately 20,000 others in Kigali,[19] RTLM congratulated its listeners. It urged them to keep up their good efforts:

> Everyone who is listening, continue your heroism,
> continue to be heroic, I think that no one has
> decided to flee. ... .[20]

In some cases, the station even suggested what types of weapons could be used. On 15 May, RTLM urged Rwandans to arm themselves with anything and everything they could find:

> Fight them with the weapons at your disposal; you
> have arrows, you have spears. ... Take up your
> traditional 'tools'.[21]

RTLM's broadcasters frequently expressed their support for people manning the roadblocks. On 8 April, Valérie Bemeriki urged:

> Let them [people at the roadblocks] be strong,
> RTLM radio is with them ... it follows them the
> whole time while ... they are at their road-blocks,
> night and day. ... that is how RTLM radio is ... it
> supports our own people.[22]

The armed forces and the militias responsible for hunting down Tutsi were a particularly important target for RTLM, which often addressed messages to them. On 22 April, Philippe Mbirizi, a Zairean journalist working for RTLM, opened in French with the following greeting: "Hello my dear friends and listeners, hello FAR, hello the whole Rwandan population, and a particular salute to those inhabitants of Kigali and elsewhere, throughout the whole country, making the nightly rounds each day".[23]

From the very beginning of the genocide, RTLM used its disc-jockey-style presentation to promote the killings. It continued to invite listeners' participation, frequently featuring interviews with studio guests, including extremist politicians, civil servants and members of the interim government, who encouraged listeners to support the security forces and assist them in fighting the "war". During May, RTLM broadcaster Gaspard Gahigi interviewed interim government Minister for the Family and Women's Affairs, Pauline Nyiramasuhuko, on the question of women's participation in the "war" effort. Nyiramasuhuko assured listeners that women in Rwanda were making significant contributions: "The Rwandan lady, like any other Rwandan, is on the front. She is fighting the RPF".[24] When asked by Gahigi why Rwandan women were not so visible in the ranks of the FAR, Nyiramasuhuko described the specific role which she claimed women were playing:

> They are not visible because there are not many of them in the Rwandan army. ... But you can see women in the civilian defence we have organized. I have seen some learning methods of fighting the enemy along with their brothers. ... Besides, when their husbands and brothers go to the front, they prepare food for them.[25]

There is little doubt that "learning methods of fighting the enemy" meant receiving instructions on how to kill. Nyiramasuhuko ended her interview saying: "I would ... like to invite Rwandan woman to work with the other Rwandans to fight the enemy."

In addition, RTLM presented interviews with supposedly random individuals who enthusiastically described their participation in the "battle" with the RPF. Gahigi used an interview with a woman named Marie-Claire Kayirange, whom he claimed was stationed at a roadblock in Muhima *secteur*, Nyarugenge *commune*, Kigali, to further encourage women to partake in genocide. The woman recounted how she was forced to flee her home and hide in a hole in the ground for three days, after her area was bombed by the RPA. She claimed, that, as a result, she became determined to help the Rwandan armed forces fight the "enemy":

> God willing I ... managed to get out [of the hole] and left. But I told myself that I would continue to fight. ... I was fighting without a gun, I did not even know how to use it, I used traditional weapons. So you see, everybody is fighting. Women ... cannot rest.[26]

Although not explicitly stated, the word "fighting" implied "killing" in this context, where genocide was continually described as war. This was reinforced by the woman's account of the means she used to counter the alleged RPF offensive. She supposedly "fought" the heavy artillery attacks by the RPF with "traditional weapons", implying that her own target could not have been military.

After joining the "battle", Kayirange claimed that she learned to fire a gun and found this useful for manning the roadblock in Muhima. She assured listeners that she was never sexually harassed by men while working at the barrier, and had only positive things to say about her experience of "fighting" for her country. When prompted by Gahigi, who asked her "what advice" she had for "the other girls", she replied: "The advice I would give the others is that they get military training and have the courage to fight the enemy". Gahigi then added, for good measure:

> She is asking the other young ladies to have the same courage and avoid the distractions of this world. 'Let us fight', she says, 'and when the war ends, those pleasures will have their time'.

The interview ended with Kayirange sending "greetings" to members of her family (see also below, section 6).

On other occasions, RTLM appeared to acknowledege that people might be hesitant about killing, but insisted that "fighting" was the only option. Kantano Habimana told his listeners they must not succumb to their fears but must be brave and engage in combat. On 13 April, he was emphatic:

> Man must to get up, adjust his *pagne* (loincloth — traditional dress) and move on. Because when the battle is there, it is there. It is no longer possible to do otherwise.[27]

Habimana claimed that this was not a battle which one could run away from; "fighting" was inevitable, there was no way around it. However, if any listeners were thinking of avoiding the responsibilities of "war",

RTLM warned of the dire consequences which they would face, reminding its audience:

> You kill him. You burn him. That happened. To a soldier who had deserted the front. If you, civilian, desert the barricade, what are they going to do if they catch you? The civilian must understand that if a soldier catches him for having deserted the barricade, he will take him to the ... *commune* authorities, to the *secteur* authorities.[28]

4   RTLM as an Instrument of Genocide: Tracking Down Individuals Trying to Escape

Beyond generally inciting genocide against the Tutsi, RTLM played a more direct role in assisting the killing. The station aided the militias and security forces in their search to identify and locate individuals targeted for elimination. All the Rwandan genocide survivors interviewed by ARTICLE 19 reported that RTLM broadcasters frequently read out names of people whom they claimed were "RPA" soldiers or "accomplices", thus marking them for extermination. In many cases, RTLM announced the precise whereabouts or even vehicle number-plates of individuals trying to hide or flee. When this occurred, the people in question were usually killed very soon thereafter, sometimes within hours of the broadcast.

Before the genocide, RTLM had mainly denounced public figures such as opposition members of the coalition government, human rights activists and journalists. These groups became the targets for assassination immediately after the genocide began, and many were killed within the first few days. During the genocide, however, RTLM shifted its focus from prominent personalities to a much wider section of Rwandans, alerting militias and security forces to people who might otherwise have remained inconspicuous, particularly in Kigali, where it was sometimes easier to hide. In several instances, RTLM appears to have played a decisive role in enabling security forces to track down and kill such individuals.

Those trying to escape constituted a major target for RTLM. The station repeatedly urged listeners to look out for people attempting to flee instead of staying to "fight" the enemy, as instructed by the authorities. According to RTLM, anyone attempting to leave an area was, consciously or unconsciously, assisting the RPA to infiltrate and should be viewed with suspicion. On 13 April, Valérie Bemeriki stated:

> You know that when they flee like that, in disarray, *Inkotanyi* find the opportunity to mingle with them. This is what we call 'infiltration' [said in French], and when they arrive somewhere, they begin to commit atrocities ... .[29]

It could be argued that this general warning constituted incitement to violence, in a context where failure to support the armed forces in their "battle against the enemy" was considered a crime punishable by death. According to RTLM, people fleeing were sometimes unwitting accomplices. On many other occasions RTLM targeted civilians more specifically, by claiming that they were RPA troops disguised as local residents. During the genocide, this claim amounted to a licence to kill anyone trying to escape. On 8 April, Bemeriki claimed: "We know that the *Inkotanyi* are now dispersing, in fact, they are spreading out amongst the inhabitants". Later in the programme, the broadcasters were more explicit, claiming that individuals, clearly fleeing for their lives, were in fact armed and dangerous. Noël Hitimana concluded: "The *Inkotanyi* have spread out into the bush ... and they are taking off for the hills ... They know how to hide and reappear!"[30]

According to witness testimony gathered by ARTICLE 19, a number of individuals travelling by car were identified and denounced by RTLM and intercepted shortly afterwards, by militias manning the roadblocks. During the first week of the genocide, RTLM described a red van which it claimed was "full of accomplices", and provided its vehicle number-plate. The passengers were family members of François Ncunguyinka, a former *préfet* of Gisenyi, fleeing to Butare, where the genocide had not yet begun. They were in Gitarama at the time of the announcement and are believed to have been halted by a roadblock in that *préfecture* the same day, and immediately executed.

Constantin Cyubaro, former Minister of Higher Education, was denounced by RTLM in April or May (ARTICLE 19's source could not provide the exact date) as he was being evacuated from Nyamirambo, Kigali, in a Red Cross ambulance, after being wounded during an incident at a roadblock in the neighbourhood. According to information received by ARTICLE 19, RTLM broadcast his name and location, and stated that he was travelling in a Red Cross vehicle. Reportedly, the ambulance was stopped en route to the centre of Kigali, near the outskirts of the city. Constantin Cyubaro was taken from the vehicle and killed by the roadside.

In a separate incident, retired FAR officer Désiré Mudenge was denounced by RTLM in April as he was trying to travel from Nyamirambo, in Kigali, to Gitarama *préfecture* in a three-car convoy of people under his protection. These included members of his family and several Tutsi. RTLM reportedly announced his name and identified the vehicles, stating that Mudenge was "a traitor" and had "accomplices with him". The convoy is believed to have been stopped almost immediately afterwards, at a roadblock near Gitega, not far from the *Office National des Transports* (National Office of Public Transport) in Kigali. Désiré Mudenge and all other members of the convoy were killed on the spot.

On 3 May, RTLM appears to have contributed to blocking the evacuation of 62 people from the Hôtel des Mille Collines which had been authorized by the interim government authorities. This five-star hotel, owned by the Belgian airline SABENA, and guarded by about a dozen UNAMIR troops, had served as a sanctuary for many Tutsi, Hutu government opponents, and foreigners, before the latter were evacuated in mid-April. UNAMIR had secured permission for the evacuation and for a FAR escort from Augustin Bizimungu, Commander-in-Chief of the army, who reportedly stated that he could not guarantee the co-operation of the militias. The attempted evacuation was highly publicized by the media, and a number of journalists were present and tried to interview the evacuees as they boarded the convoy. According to witnesses, RTLM journalist Ananie Nkurunziza also observed the evacuation, from outside the Hotel. Immediately after the evacuees had entered the buses, RTLM reportedly broadcast the full names of all 62 people and directed the militias to attack the convoy. Two buses were stopped at separate roadblocks. Several people from the first bus were ordered out of the vehicle and beaten. They were able to escape when a skirmish broke out amongst the security forces manning the roadblock. The second bus was permitted to return to the hotel after UNAMIR radioed for help and Colonel Tharcisse Renzaho and Georges Rutaganda, Second Vice-President of the *Interahamwe*, intervened.

In a separate incident in April or May 1994, François-Xavier Nsanzuwera reported to ARTICLE 19 that he heard RTLM provide full details of a vehicle in Nyamirambo which it claimed contained *"Inyenzi"*. The car belonged to Alain Mudenge, son of a former Rwandan Ambassador to the UN. He and Désiré Nshunguyinka, whose father had formerly served as a government minister and as a *préfet*, were travelling with members of their respective families. They were apparently spotted in Nyamirambo and immediately killed. Shortly afterwards, RTLM announced that their initial broadcast about the car had in fact been a mistake.

In some instances, RTLM broadcasters issued "corrections" about individuals whom they had denounced, in time to prevent them from facing certain death. During the first three weeks of the genocide, a caller appears to have provided RTLM with the vehicle number-plate of Emmanuel Nkunduwimye, brother-in-law of RPF supporter Silas Majyambere, which the radio then broadcast, claiming that he, too, supported the RPF. However, Emmanuel Nkunduwimye subsequently convinced members of the security forces that he backed the interim government, not the RPF. RTLM broadcasters issued a correction and told listeners that this man was, in fact, "one of their own". Nkunduwimye was then permitted to travel freely, and later accompanied a woman, very much at risk, to safety in Zaire. Half Tutsi, and the wife of a well-known journalist, she had been targeted from the beginning of the genocide.

The fact that RTLM issued "corrections" about specific individuals, having denounced them earlier, underlines the importance of the station's role in identifying people for the security forces and militias. Moreover, its influence on the militias during the genocide was emphasized by an unusual case in which RTLM appears to have helped free a man who had been taken hostage by militia members. A 39-year-old car mechanic was abducted by militia members from Biryogo around 5.00 a.m. on 30 April. He was freed after people from his area pressured RTLM to broadcast an announcement stating that he should be released.

RTLM's close relationship to the militias during the genocide period is also demonstrated by a case reported to ARTICLE 19 involving the head of the gendarmerie, General Augustin Ndindiliyimana, who, in mid-April, was accused by RTLM of transporting RPA soldiers when, he claims, he was trying to evacuate several Tutsi civilians. RTLM broadcast a description of his vehicle and its number-plate. The General reported that, despite his formal position, he felt threatened and immediately changed cars on hearing the broadcast.

5   Directing Militias to Places of Hiding and Refuge

RTLM provided a significant amount of information as to the whereabouts of specific individuals who were trying to hide from the militias and security forces and encouraged listeners to phone in with any details they had about "RPA" soldiers and their "accomplices". It also played an important role in directing militias to places of refuge, where larger numbers of people were located.

On 10 April 1994, Valérie Bemeriki read out 13 names of people she claimed were "RPF leaders" in various areas of Kigali. In addition, she provided their addresses, jobs, nicknames and, in some cases, the places they were said to frequent. Bemeriki alleged that these individuals were conspiring to assassinate political figures in Rwanda, and stated that "security" could not be re-established until they were found. She called upon her listeners to immediately locate them.

In most cases, however, RTLM did not provide such complete profiles of targeted individuals, generally announcing the name or simply the neighbourhood of persons it claimed were "*Inyenzi*". Providing the location often proved sufficient to provoke an attack by local militias within a few hours. As one survivor of the genocide explained:

> RTLM often stated: 'We have just learned that
> so-and-so has ammunition'. This was the way to
> point him out. The next day, the militia would be at
> his house.[31]

According to journalist Sixbert Musangamfura, RTLM broadcasters criticized the militias if they failed to carry out attacks on particular individuals. Musangamfura explained that Kantano Habimana would announce:

> I have just learned that the people who went to his
> place did not find him. Where could he be? Con-
> tinue to search the area.[32]

When only a name was announced, it was usually insufficient information to immediately pinpoint the victim. Nevertheless, it alerted people manning the extensive roadblocks throughout the country, who were checking identity cards. Thus, in a number of such cases, individuals who were denounced by RTLM were eventually killed within several days of the broadcast.

One of the most prominent people targeted by the station in this way was the wealthy businessman Antoine Sebera, a Tutsi. He was mentioned several times by RTLM in early April and accused of hiding large quantities of firearms and RPA troops at his estate in Gikondo, Kigali. Several witnesses interviewed by ARTICLE 19 reported hearing RTLM call upon its listeners to attack his home. On 8 April 1994, Valérie Bemeriki warned:

> the little *Inyenzi* ... even if they were still hoping to
> be guests of Sebera and find security in his cellar
> ... now they are being grilled right there ... now
> they are burning. ... In fact, there was a fair number
> of 'little things' [RPA troops] ... crowded in there
> [the cellar].[33]

Antoine Sebera often hunted game, and possessed a number of firearms specifically for this activity for which he, reportedly, had the necessary papers. He is not believed to have been involved with the

RPF, but he had been detained for one week during the massive arrests of October 1990, before being released without charge. According to RTLM, however, he was an RPF leader and his home or, more specifically, his cellar (*cave*) was described as a major strategic point for the rebels. Although RTLM did not give numbers, Bemeriki insinuated that an entire RPF battalion could be stationed there; she claimed there were so many RPA troops in his house that "people would think it an exaggeration" if she were to announce the actual figure.

Embellishing this presumably fictitious account of an RPF stronghold, Bemeriki claimed that the Rwandan security forces already had the situation under control. Antoine Sebera and his allies were, she claimed: "being grilled ... burnt". A few minutes later, she again mentioned Sebera, this time in passing, and maintained that the attack on his home was a *fait accompli*. Extolling the virtues of the FAR and their victory over the evil enemy, she referred to "the little *Inkotanyi* which we crushed at Sebera's place".

According to André Sebera, Antoine Sebera's son, who spoke to his father on the telephone from Brussels during the days before he was murdered, and who has since investigated the circumstances of his father's death, the attack on the house did not begin until the following morning. At around 11.00 a.m. on Saturday 9 April, security forces began to throw grenades at the house and Antoine Sebera and his family reportedly resisted, using the firearms kept for hunting. On Monday 11 April, Antoine Sebera phoned RTLM and insisted that he was not harbouring any RPA troops in his home. Apparently, he pleaded with RTLM broadcasters to correct what they had said, and told them to come and see for themselves if in doubt. Later in the day, RTLM broadcasters discussed, on air, the conversation they had with Antoine Sebera, but still maintained he was hiding rebels. On Tuesday, the attacks on the house intensified and Sebera and his family retreated to the cellar. During the night of 12-13 April, after militias shelled the house, which caught fire, Antoine Sebera, four family members and four other people who had been hiding, fled the premises. According to one witness, they managed to reach the front of the Canadian Embassy but were refused entry. As Sebera and his family were reportedly still armed with hunting guns, the militias and police protecting the Embassy called for reinforcements from the FAR, who arrived shortly afterwards, and shot him, his family, and the other four people dead.[34]

RTLM also accused others of active involvement in arming and fighting alongside the RPF. In the particularly wealthy area of Kivugiza, part of Nyamirambo, where many Tutsi lived, a man named Joseph Kahabaye was reportedly singled out in this way by Noël Hitimana, who also lived there. During the first few days of the genocide, Hitimana did not criticize people in this area but, instead, reported that all was well there, saying, "At Kivugiza, we stand together". Around 11 or 12 April, however, Hitimana claimed that this entire area was a centre of RPF activity, alleged that Joseph Kahabaye was responsible, and reportedly said: "in our area, at Kivugiza, a lot of arms have been distributed ... Kahabaye's house is a bastion of the RPF. ... People from the RPF are hiding in the attics". The entire area was raided by militias within hours of the broadcast and Joseph Kahabaye was killed. The militias continued to attack Kivugiza for the next few days until all the Tutsi there were slaughtered.

In another case, on the morning of 16 April, PSD leader Dr Théoneste Gafaranga was tracked down and killed just a few hours after RTLM repeatedly broadcast that there was "a big *Inyenzi*" still left in the neighbourhood of Rugenge, Kigali. Dr Gafaranga had been hiding in the area, not far from his home, since 7 April, and was the last PSD leader left alive; the others had been assassinated in the first days of the genocide. According to witnesses, RTLM addressed the militias specifically and directed them to the area with the following message:

> Urgent! urgent! calling the militia members of
> Muhima! Direct yourselves to the Rugenge area ...
> we have been informed that the *Inyenzi* and their
> accomplices have not yet returned to the CND.

The militias searched the neighbourhood until, at 11.30 a.m., they found Dr Gafaranga, a well-known personality. They arrested him and took him away immediately. The RPF station, Radio Muhabura, announced news of his death just a few hours later.

On 15 April, Charles Kalinijabo, a Tutsi, was denounced by RTLM which provided both his name and location. According to witness testimony, RTLM stated: "there are accomplices who are walking around the barriers of Nyamirambo, one of whom is Charles Kalinijabo ..." Kalinijabo had been helping to man a roadblock in Nyamirambo when the broadcast, apparently, prompted local militias to search him out. He was immediately arrested, taken to his home and executed there.

Meanwhile, journalist and priest André Sibomana, Editor of the independent Catholic newspaper *Kinyamateka*, reported that RTLM broadcast information about him when he was hiding in the Centre Saint Paul in Kigali. According to Father Sibomana, on the morning of 12 April, the station broadcast that there was "a high-level accomplice" hiding in the Centre but did not provide his name. After hearing this announcement, he immediately fled the premises. At 2.00 p.m., several militia members arrived at the Centre looking for him.[35]

Civil servants who resisted instructions to order the massacres were also denounced by RTLM. Justin Nyandwi, then *bourgemestre* of Musambira *commune*, reported that on 10 April he, his driver and three local policemen, were threatened by *Interahamwe*, led by Rose Karushara of Kimisagara, Kigali, after he had directed people in his area to prevent the *Interahamwe* from entering the *commune*. They were saved when Kigali City's Chief of Police, Major Nyamuhimba, intervened. According to Nyandwi, on 14 April, RTLM announced that he should be eliminated because he opposed the massacres. On 20 April, a large group of *Interahamwe* went to his house, searching for him, but he and his family escaped. In a separate case, Callixte Ndagijimana, *bourgemestre* of Mugina, was caught and executed on 20 April. He also had been targeted by RTLM, a few days previously, for trying to protect people in his administrative division.

By many accounts, the *préfet* of Butare, Jean-Baptiste Habyarimana, had been instrumental in preventing killings in Butare, which was the last area in Rwanda to experience the genocide. The only Tutsi *préfet* in Rwanda, Habyarimana also took measures to protect the internally displaced from other *préfectures* who sought refuge in Butare. On 13 April, when the Butare *préfecture* had still not experienced any killings, Valérie Bemeriki accused Jean-Baptiste Habyarimana of working for the RPF and warned listeners:

> I have told you, persistently, the *Inkotanyi* claimed
> they would make a breakthrough in Gitarama and
> in Butare ... especially in Butare ... where they
> would find an opening. And we are aware of the
> fact that they have accomplices everywhere – even
> the *préfet* of Butare – and I am not making this up,
> he himself said that he is a member of the PL but
> that, when the RPF comes, he will become a fol-
> lower of the RPF. So, if he plans to become an RPF
> supporter, that means that he is already working
> for the RPF.[36]

Bemeriki identified Butare and Gitarama *préfectures* as key points of
strategic importance for the RPF. She claimed to have received
indications from the RPF that it planned to attack from these
préfectures. This was, obviously, entirely untrue since the RPF led its
offensive from the north, where most of its troops had been stationed
since before the genocide. Bemeriki warned her listeners to remain
vigilant, insisting that there were "accomplices everywhere". She
implied that the *préfet* himself had informed her that he was an RPF
supporter.

On 18 April, five days after this broadcast, Jean-Baptiste
Habyarimana was dismissed by the interim government, which also
purged other civil servants in Butare for opposing the genocide.
Habyarimana was last seen in Butare City the day he was sacked; he is
believed to have spent one week in hiding before being arrested, taken
to Gitarama, capital of the interim government, and summarily
executed. Massacres began in Butare *préfecture* on the day of his
dismissal and included some of the worst in the entire period of
genocide.[37]

Another group targeted by RTLM was priests believed to be
protecting or hiding people in their churches or parishes. During the
genocide, many church leaders demonstrated a high level of
complicity with the interim authorities. Priests who resisted the
massacres, therefore, took extraordinary risks. RTLM often
accused such priests of being RPA troops or of supporting the RPF
offensive. On 20 May 1994, Valérie Bemeriki accused Father Pierre

Ngoga of slaughtering Hutu, describing a presumably fictitious account of an attack in Kibeho, Gikongoro *préfecture*:

> There were 88 Tutsi who were going to commit the irreparable. ... This backfired when Father Ngoga took a rifle, positioned himself near the church and began shooting at the Hutu ... while they were chasing these Tutsi who came to attack them. People saw it. ... He took his car and fled. ... Even today, he is still on the loose.[38]

According to many witnesses interviewed by African Rights, Father Pierre Ngoga had tried to protect people in his parish from the security forces during April and May. He was killed in Butare about ten days after this broadcast, on 31 May. The church in Kibeho was burned down and the thousands of refugees within were massacred. Bemeriki cited a number of other priests whom she accused of similar atrocities. She continued: "Father Ngoga is not alone. How about Muvara? ... Can Father Ntagara explain to Rwandans why the Eucharist has been replaced with ammunition?"[39] Two priests, named Augustin Ntagara and Félicien Muvura, had already been killed on 7 and 29 April, respectively.

Beyond singling out specific priests and parishioners, RTLM also targeted churches and other places where large numbers of displaced persons were hiding or hoping to find refuge. At the beginning of the genocide, RTLM claimed that RPA troops were using churches throughout the country as military bases, thereby encouraging attacks on churches, where some of the largest massacres in Rwanda took place, often with thousands killed at a time.[40] Never before in Rwanda had churches been so systematically violated. On 8 April, Noël Hitimana told listeners that "a Doctor" had given him the following advice:

> he said 'during these times in which we are living ... if you have to see people seeking refuge in the parish churches ... and in other places ... this is not good at all' ... he said 'moreover you find that these people ... whom they [RPA troops] have placed in the parish churches and elsewhere. ... [were] ...

given them grenades and other arms ... all this is
not good.[41]

Hitimana tried to make this outrageous claim appear authoritative by citing the "Doctor" as his source, a man whom he described as "someone I really trust".[42]

On 7 April, the day after the Presidential plane had been shot down, an estimated 200-300 people fled to the church at Nyamirambo, in Kigali. Later that day, a small number of militia members tried forcibly to enter the church, but many of those hiding formed a barricade and, using traditional weapons, resisted the incursion. Witnesses reported to ARTICLE 19 that, throughout the night of 7-8 April, RTLM repeatedly broadcast that the church was full of armed RPA troops and announced that reinforcements were required. At 10.00 a.m. on 8 April, a truck full of security forces arrived and stormed the church grounds, forced people out of the church and shot dead about 60 persons. Many others fled.

A number of those who escaped the massacre in the Nyamirambo church hid in the nearby Collège Saint André. There, a similar siege occurred following another broadcast by RTLM. By 11 April, an estimated 100 people were hiding in the school. According to witness testimony, RTLM targeted the school on 11 or 12 April, claiming it was harbouring RPF accomplices. In apparent response to the RTLM broadcast, on the evening of 13 April, the RPF rescued about 40 of the people hiding there. On 14 or 15 April, militias stormed the premises and killed all those remaining.

A similar case occurred on 10 April, when RTLM directed militias to attack hundreds of people who were sheltering in the Nyamirambo Mosque. According to lawyer Frédéric Mutagwera, interviewed by African Rights:

> RTLM complained that this Mosque, which it named, was full of refugees. On Monday and Tuesday, soldiers and *Interahamwe* came to the Mosque, shooting in all directions. RTLM, which passed on the message, is directly responsible for inciting this particular massacre.[43]

Approximately 300 people, mostly Tutsi, were killed.

In mid-June, towards the end of the genocide, RTLM appears to have played a role in ordering a raid on the Church of St Famille, in Rugenge *secteur*, Nyarugenge *commune*, where large numbers of people had sought refuge since April. It was located next to the Centre St Paul, which also served as a sanctuary during the genocide. On 14 June, at least 42 men were specifically selected and taken from St Paul's by *Interahamwe*, allegedly on the orders of a Rugenge councillor, Odette Nyirabagenzi. During the night of 16 June, the RPF organized a raid to evacuate those sheltering in St Paul's and St Famille's and succeeded in rescuing 1,800 from St Paul's but failed to gain entry to St Famille.[44] Witnesses reported to ARTICLE 19 that, early the following morning, RTLM called for an attack on St Famille, claiming that it was still harbouring "accomplices". Later that day, militias stormed St Famille and executed approximately 100 men.

6 Military Radio

Beyond addressing the general public, RTLM appears to have largely focused on the more specific audience of the security forces and militias. Despite its repeated orders for all "citizens" to partake in the genocide, it was this latter group of military and paramilitary organizations, rather than the population, which orchestrated and carried out large-scale massacres throughout the country at a relentless pace. In addition to targeting individuals and groups of people for the militias, RTLM appears to have relayed inside information about military developments to militia members and FAR troops, at least in Kigali.[45] Many observers believe that RTLM had a direct link or radio connection to high-ranking members of the security forces because it frequently conveyed up to the minute information about the situation in combat zones.

On several occasions, RTLM broadcast requests from civil servants or militia leaders for supplies of weapons and ammunition to be delivered to their areas. Gaspard Gahigi interviewed a woman named Euphrasia Kamatamu, councillor for Muhima *secteur*, Nyarugenge *commune*, Kigali, who stated:

> Concerning the weapons, because we are directly
> facing the enemy, we need more than the other
> sectors. ... the civilians ... would have [more
> strength] by getting more weapons, because nobody
> would be afraid if all had their weapons".[46]

Kamatamu has been accused by African Rights of playing a role in organizing the killing by militias in her area.[47] Another interviewee, Marie-Claire Kayirange, who claimed to be manning a roadblock in this same area, also indicated that additional weapons were needed. At the very end of her studio visit, Gahigi announced: "Kayirange says there is a shortage of guns at the barricades. The councillor and the others in charge will look into the problem".[48]

This use of the station to broadcast information specifically destined for the military and militias is demonstrated by the interrogation of Janvier Salongo, a captured RPA soldier, which RTLM broadcast live on 15 April 1994. This 20-year-old Rwandan exile had lived in Zaire since childhood and had barely set foot in Rwanda before the genocide. He was taken prisoner by the FAR after being left behind by members of an RPA battalion in Kigali following a battle. Salongo was subjected to a lengthy interrogation by four FAR officers who bombarded him with questions about the RPF and its strategic plans for the war. Clearly disorientated, with his voice faltering at many points during the cross-examination, the young soldier seemed for the most part genuinely unable, although at times unwilling, to answer their insistent questions. The interrogation continued:

> FAR: ... why did you chose Gikondo [neighbour-
> hood in Kigali — for the attack]?
> JS: Gikondo? Gikondo, I don't even know where it
> is ... it is like I was taken around without knowing
> where I was going.
> FAR: In fact when you go on the hills [for an
> attack], you go in groups of what size?
> JS: On the hills? We went out on the hills in a
> platoon.
> FAR: How many men are in a platoon?
> JS: 30 ... but not all platoons are the same.

FAR: What distinguishes them?
JS: Some have a lot and others have few.
FAR: ... and afterwards ... when you [the RPF] leave here ... what are your plans after that ... after Rebero [strategic point in South Kigali taken by RPF troops]?
JS: Our plans are to fight. Period!
FAR: To fight where?

Bringing the captured soldier to the RTLM studio and exposing him to listeners no doubt served to bolster the interim government's claim that they were winning the war against the rebels. It also publicly humiliated the RPF, given that his fellow platoon members had left him behind enemy lines, but was more than just a public relations exercise. Salongo's interrogators attempted to extract information which could assist the FAR in repulsing the RPA offensive. The FAR officers continually pressured the soldier to reveal details about the RPA which were so specific that they would have been incomprehensible to anyone not directly engaged in combat.

The incessant questions continued relating to the targets the RPA were planning to attack next, and how the rebels generally decided which areas to target. The FAR officers asked where the men in Salongo's battalion had gone, and how many men were in his unit. In addition, they tried to find out more general information, including what the command structure was for the RPA's battle units, and how the RPF acquired arms and ammunition. They also asked how many men the RPA had lost in battles with the FAR since the start of the genocide. During their exchanges with the soldier, the FAR officers made no wild accusations of fictitious rebel atrocities, as RTLM broadcasters had consistently done. Perhaps they did not want to give Salongo the opportunity to refute such allegations. They did, however, maintain that the RPF had killed President Habyarimana and demanded that Salongo explain why the RPF had done this. He responded by weakly stating that he knew nothing about any RPF involvement in the crash.

In general, their manner was direct, their questions were factual, and they largely refrained from taunting Salongo on air. On occasion, they indulged in making ironic comments. After asking Salongo to explain how he came to be captured, one officer commented: "don't you see that they [RPA troops] have hurt you?". The soldier sadly admitted his bewilderment at having been abandoned under these circumstances: "me too, that is what ... I ... I thought about why they did this and I didn't understand it myself". Janvier Salongo is presumed to have been killed by the Rwandan security forces following the broadcast.

7 RTLM Versus Radio Rwanda

From the very beginning of the genocide, the RPF argued that RTLM was playing a pernicious role in the massacres and repeatedly called for it to be shut down. On 16 April, the RPF demanded the immediate closure of the station as one of four preconditions to any negotiations with the interim government authorities.[49] This was ignored and the RPA shelled the RTLM station around noon the following day. RTLM was broadcasting live at the time of the attack and witnesses reported to ARTICLE 19 that they listened to the shelling on the radio as well as the reactions of the broadcasters as they realized what was happening. The broadcast continued for about 30 minutes after the bombing, during which time listeners heard RTLM journalists assessing the damage. According to *Médecins sans frontières*, Valérie Bemeriki and Noël Hitimana suffered serious injuries and were evacuated to the Centre Hospitalier de Kigali, run by the Red Cross. Bemeriki had to have a leg amputated but is still alive.

After shutting down for about three hours, RTLM reportedly re-launched its programmes later that day by triumphantly and defiantly announcing that nothing could stop them because "you cannot extinguish the voice of the 'numerous' people [meaning Hutu]". After this attack, RTLM is believed to have moved to a mobile station. African Rights reported that the radio relocated to "an armored vehicle supplied, manned and protected by Presidential Guards".[50]

RTLM continued to operate regularly but no longer broadcast for 24 hours a day and the range of its broadcasts appears to have diminished. Later, on 4 July, after the RPF took control of Kigali, the station went off the air and relocated to Gisenyi *préfecture*, where the interim government moved on 12 July. RTLM is reported to have begun broadcasting again on 10 July. It went off the air one week later.

The BBC Monitoring Service in Nairobi was able to pick up Radio Rwanda broadcasts only during the first five days of the genocide. After 12 April, it appears to have stopped broadcasting on its short wave frequency, apparently because the relay station it shared with Deutsche Welle near Kigali was damaged when fighting between the FAR and RPA reached the surrounding area. Radio Rwanda is believed to have broadcast throughout the rest of the genocide on FM frequency, with a reduced range.

During the first few days of the genocide, Minister of Information, Faustin Rucogoza, was assassinated and Director of ORINFOR, Jean-Marie Vianney Higiro, fled the country. Both were MDR party members who had tried to introduce reforms and improve the independence of Radio Rwanda's reporting. Eliézer Niyitegeka, from the extremist "Hutu Power" faction of the MDR, was appointed Minister of Information; Jean-Baptiste Bamwanga, Radio Rwanda journalist and RTLM shareholder, became Director of ORINFOR; Another RTLM founder, Froduald Ntawulikura, was retained by Radio Rwanda which underwent a purge, as many of its moderate journalists were killed, while several alleged extremists, such as Jean-Baptiste Nubahumpatse, a local stringer for the BBC French for Africa Service, were promoted.[51]

After 7 April, Radio Rwanda served as a mouthpiece for interim government officials including from the Ministry of Defence, who made a number of official announcements, informing the public about curfews and travel restrictions. Gérard Prunier writes that, in contrast to RTLM, the government station initially "remained neutral and confined itself to information bulletins".[52]

Over the next number of weeks, Radio Rwanda reportedly became more vehement, serving as a platform for extremist politicians and interim government authorities, who frequently gave lengthy interviews or speeches in which they incited genocide. Unlike their counterparts at RTLM, Radio Rwanda journalists do not appear to have used these interviews as background to their own elaborate commentaries. Moreover, Radio Rwanda does not appear to have played an active role in the killings. It neither directed militias to specific locations nor assisted them in tracking down particular individuals.

The station did, however, incite genocide by calling upon people to assist the security forces in "defending" the nation. It also generally requested people to remain vigilant and help track down the "enemy". A broadcast in French on 12 April advised listeners:

> The people should not panic, but tell the security forces where the enemy is hiding. This happened in the Gikondo Sector yesterday when the attention of a patrol of the national gendarmerie was drawn to the presence of seven RPF combatants hiding in a house.[53]

8   Speeches and Announcements by the Interim Authorities

The initial speeches by interim government President Théodore Sindikubwabo and Prime Minister Jean Kambanda, during the very first days of the genocide, were formal pronouncements on the composition and aims of the new government, which were probably intended to make it appear legitimate. Although the self-proclaimed government had effectively come to power through a *coup d'état*, Théodore Sindikubwabo insinuated that he and his cabinet of MRND, CDR and extremist "Hutu Power" faction leaders, had assumed power legally. On 9 April, Sindikubwabo spoke of "the death of the President of the Republic [which] was unfortunately followed by other tragic events during which other people, such as Prime Minister Agathe Uwilingiyimana, died".[54] He also expressed the "sincere condolences of the Rwandan government and people to the bereaved families" of these figures.[55]

At a press conference the next day, Prime Minister Kambanda elaborated on what he claimed were the reasons for the killings of former government members:

> There have been confrontations among the population, especially in the city of Kigali, and people have been killed, including the Prime Minister,

Madame Agathe Uwilingiyimana, and some
ministers as well as several citizens.[56]

He asserted that the population, overwhelmed with grief at the death
of their President, had suddenly become violent. The assassinations of
Prime Minister Agathe Uwilingiyimana and other ministers were
supposedly the result of this surge in random violence. He repeated,
several times, that this was the only possible explanation for the killings which had swept Kigali, insisting:

> ... it is largely this which has led to this turmoil;
> our wish is that people try to understand this. ...
> that people understand the reasons which have
> provoked acts of violence of such a scale.[57]

These two figures spoke in general terms about the measures they
claimed were needed to "restore security", but did not provide
specific instructions as to how citizens were expected to help. In his
inaugural speech to parliament on 9 April, President Sindikubwabo
applauded the security forces, which by then had already carried out
widespread killings in the capital:

> I would ... like to thank and give support to our
> country's forces who acted swiftly after the death
> of the President and did their utmost, as always, to
> preserve the peace of Rwandans, especially here
> in the capital.[58]

In addition, Sindikubwabo praised the army for its plans to establish a
"crisis committee" together with "civilian leaders", to deal with the
situation at hand.

In his speech to parliament the same day, Prime Minister
Kambanda also indicated that the government and security forces would
address the situation, but did not explain how. He simply assured
citizens that "the Ministers of Defence, of Communal Development,
and of Justice, will do everything possible to restore peace as soon as
possible, let us say within about two weeks".

RTLM and the Genocide

In contrast to the general statements by Sindikubwabo and Kambanda, from the very beginning of the genocide, civil servants issued specific orders which the civilian population was expected to follow. On 8 April, the *sous-préfet* of Kigali, François Karera, made the following announcement on RTLM:

> The *préfet* of Kigali asks all citizens to continue to be vigilant so that, together with the army, they can defend the integrity of our country. Citizens, in collaboration with their local authorities, the "ten-houses",[59] the heads of *cellules*, communal councillors, *bourgemestres*, and even party leaders, must mobilize to secure their *cellules* and *secteurs* so that they can unmask any person hiding in their midst intending to support the enemy.[60]

This official statement made it clear to what extent citizens were required to participate in efforts to "restore order". Their role was as important as that of the armed forces; the civilians were expected to work "together with the army". This announcement also indicates how the role of civil servants, throughout the country, proved decisive during the genocide period. The entire administrative apparatus was instructed to become involved in the genocide. The *bourgemestres,* political party leaders, *responsables de cellules*, down to the leaders of the 'dix-maison' units, required the local population to "mobilize" to assist in the killing. The *sous-préfet* went on to explain precisely what this "mobilization" would entail:

> For this reason they [citizens] need to keep a watch on all roads and, moreover, wherever the enemy is suspected to be hiding – wherever this is – flush him out without restraint. People are asked not to abandon their homes, as this would give an opening to the enemy. They are asked to patrol and to heed Radio Rwanda.[61]

These instructions were precise. People throughout Kigali *préfecture* were delegated responsibility for hunting down "the enemy" in their particular neighbourhoods. People were not told to look for an invading guerrilla army, nor even for individuals who were armed or seemed dangerous. Instead, they were asked to target all individuals found hiding. No evidence nor sign of RPF involvement was necessary; the Tutsi generally were tacitly associated with the RPF troops.

Several days later, both Sindikubwabo and Kambanda were more explicit in their speeches, and openly called for the general population to participate in the genocide or "final war". They travelled to Butare *préfecture* on 19 April, the day that Tutsi *préfet* Jean-Baptiste Habyarimana was dismissed along with other members of the administration in that *préfecture* for opposing the genocide. There had been no killings in Butare until then. On 21 April, Sindikubwabo and Kambanda gave particularly vehement speeches in Butare in which they attacked both the administrative authorities and the population in the area for having refused to carry out the genocide. Jean Kambanda addressed a gathering in Butare:

> ... All of us, together, must wage this war ... it is a final war, it must be finished. I address this message to certain *bourgemestres* who, it has been reported to me, have gone to train with the *Inkotanyi* ... they [the *bourgemestres*] should make them [the RPF] understand that the government is determined. The State, the military, the people have decided to wage this war, and to win it.[62]

The Prime Minister employed the terminology of genocide as the "final war", which had been used by RTLM consistently from 7 April onwards. He emphasized the need for the entire population, including the administrative authorities in all the *préfectures*, to contribute. By singling out the *bourgemestres* in Butare and accusing them of working with the RPF, he immediately targeted them for killing.

Meanwhile, Sindikubwabo addressed his speech to the entire population of Butare. Although he discussed the responsibility of civil servants in the genocide, he, too, underlined the need for all civilians to give their full "participation":

> During these difficult periods, our wish is that the [security] forces be assisted by all able-bodied members of the population; all, all of us. Let no one say 'this does not concern me'. ... Security is not a matter for the gendarmes alone; security is a matter which, above all, affects the population; the gendarmes only intervene afterwards, when the population encounters insurmountable difficulties.[63]

For Sindikubwabo, there could be no exceptions; the general security of the country was a matter which concerned the population at large and, therefore, had to be dealt with by everyone, not simply the security forces. People themselves needed to take responsibility for "fighting" and should only look to the security forces in case of "difficulties". He warned that any person who refused or failed to co-operate would be severely punished. Any such individuals should be denounced and brought before the authorities to "explain" why they did not feel an obligation to partake in the genocide, why "they do not feel that this affects them".[64]

9 On RTLM: The Journalists and Interim Government Officials Respond

During the genocide and after the fall of the interim government on 18 July, RTLM journalists publicly denied that they played any role whatsoever in inciting violence. The interim government officials, however, did not refute the charge that RTLM incited violence but repeatedly stated that it was a private radio station over which they had no control. Both groups have since argued that what occurred in Rwanda from April to July 1994 was not genocide.

In early May 1994, the Belgian RTLM announcer Georges Ruggiu sent a fax to Radio-Télévision Belgique Francophone (RTBF) in which he refuted allegations that he engaged in incitement to violence against either Belgian or Rwandan nationals while working at RTLM. Earlier, on 18 April, the Belgian Minister of Justice, Melchior Wathelet, had requested an investigation to determine whether Georges Ruggiu should be charged with incitement to commit crimes. Interviewed in Zaire in August 1994, Ruggiu claimed that RTLM never violated the law. He stated:

> We did not incite racial hatred. We did incite people to be critical about the RPF and some interpreted that as a call to kill Tutsis [*sic*]. But we never pronounced the word 'Tutsi'. ... It was a station where people dared to say what they thought. But I defy anyone to find a tape of me saying: 'You must kill'. ... It's not true to say we told falsehoods or called on people to kill each other. We simply said the RPF did not want peace.[65]

From the evidence of available recordings of RTLM broadcasts during the genocide, it is quite possible that Georges Ruggiu never literally called on listeners to "kill Tutsi", as he claimed. RTLM did imply that the "RPF" meant the Tutsi generally; perhaps it is not surprising that Ruggiu pointed to this use of language to support his claim. However, evidence that the station incited genocide is overwhelming, regardless of the particular terms which RTLM employed.

RTLM journalists Emmanuel Rucogoza and Gaspard Gahigi also denied that the station ever broadcast anything that was not totally accurate. According to Rucogoza, RTLM was controversial precisely because "this radio tells the truth and the truth hurts".[66] In an interview with ARTICLE 19 in Goma, Zaire, Gahigi maintained that there was long-standing tension between Hutu and Tutsi in Rwanda and that RTLM simply reported on this "problem" but did nothing to exacerbate it. He mocked the notion that RTLM could have had any responsibility for what happened during the genocide period:

> Is a journalist who talks about a problem which really exists and threatens society ... guilty for having said it or, rather, would he be guilty for not

having said it? ... Since all the media, worldwide,
are now unanimous in recognizing that, in Rwanda,
there is an ethnic problem which led to the human
catastrophe which we see today, if RTLM had not
said it, would this have prevented the problem from
existing?[67]

Gahigi insinuated that the allegations of incitement to violence stemmed
from the station's coverage of the supposed "ethnic problem" in
Rwanda. He glossed over the question of incitement, claiming that
RTLM was being criticized because it dared to report on this taboo
issue. Ironically, he was able to bolster his claim by pointing to the
fact that the international media have frequently explained the Rwandan
genocide as a situation of ethnic conflict. He concluded by insisting
that RTLM had merely become the victim of RPF propaganda:

... by telling the truth, by exposing the truth about
the RPF. ... [the RPF] began to wage anti-RTLM
propaganda. This is why RTLM has now found
itself, even before we left the country ... the pet
hate of the RPF.[68]

During the genocide, the interim government officials did not go to
any lengths to defend the content of RTLM broadcasts, instead they
repeatedly claimed that the station was exercising its legitimate right
to freedom of expression. When asked about RTLM by US
Congressman Dan Burton, the Rwandan Ambassador to the US
replied, "It is a private radio station which the government does not
control".[69] On 16 April 1994, Rwandan government spokespersons
also used this argument to respond to criticisms of the station by the
international media. When questioned by RTBF about its anti-Belgian
campaign, the Rwandan Foreign Minister responded:

The burgeoning of the democratic press in Rwanda
was accompanied by the birth of private media
organizations, which by definition are beyond the
government's control. The reality is as much a fact
in Rwanda as it is in Belgium.[70]

He argued that, if disturbed by RTLM's allegations, the Belgian government could take steps such as "making use of its right of reply" or issuing public statements to deny what the station had broadcast.[71]

The interim government Minister of Information, Eliézer Niyitegeka, also claimed that RTLM respected the right of reply and that any listeners could have used it during the genocide to correct what had been said about them. He also argued that he had no control over the station. In December 1994, he explained:

> RTLM was an independent station. Anyway, nobody complained about RTLM except the UN Commander, General Dallaire, who didn't like what was said about him. I asked RTLM to offer him airtime for his views and they did. If others had complained, they could have had time to put their view.[72]

10   The Reaction of the International Community: The Decision Not to Jam RTLM

Despite the role of RTLM in inciting genocide and the lobbying efforts of international human rights groups, Western governments appear to have failed to seriously consider the possibility of jamming RTLM. From the very beginning of the genocide the US Committee on Refugees consistently lobbied the US government to jam RTLM, but the United States initially refused, arguing that it would have been too technologically difficult and would have represented a violation of international law. Jeff Drumtra, Africa Policy Analyst for the US Committee on Refugees, reported that over a month later, he was contacted by a representative of the US State Department who told him that the US was considering jamming RTLM, but could not locate its frequency. The US Committee on Refugees was able to find this information within two hours and immediately relayed it to the US government representative. The United States, however, failed to take any steps to stop RTLM broadcasting. George Moose, Assistant

Secretary of State for African Affairs, reported on 4 May that the US had the capacity to jam RTLM, saying, "we probably would have gone forward with [the jamming] but in the meantime we learned that the RPF had successfully shelled [RTLM]". He claimed that the station was no longer broadcasting.

Nor did the French government attempt to jam RTLM after its troops landed in Rwanda for *Opération Turquoise* and established safe-haven zones in early July. The mission had been authorized by the UN Security Council [Resolution 929 (1994)] as a "strictly humanitarian" operation.[73] By early July, French soldiers had gained control of Gikongoro, Cyangugu and Kibuye in south-west Rwanda. According to François Léotard, French Minister of Defence, the French government did not consider the possibility of jamming RTLM because this was not part of its mandate as agreed by the UN.[74] On 2 July 1994, French Foreign Ministry spokesperson Catherine Colonna reported that RTLM had ceased broadcasting, but did not specify what exactly had happened. She provided assurances that the station would never have been allowed to operate within the *Opération Turquoise* area:

> We had specified ... that if these radio stations [Radio Rwanda and RTLM] were in our zone, measures would be taken to ensure that they stopped broadcasting.[75]

The issue of RTLM was finally raised by the UN Security Council on 27 June 1994, a few weeks before the RPF took over the country, marking the end of the genocide. A number of member state representatives criticized the station for its attacks against both Tutsi civilians and UNAMIR troops, but no formal measures were taken to ensure that it be closed down. The president of the UN Security Council, Salim Bin Mohammed Al-Khussaiby of Oman, stated that "such comments against UNAMIR will not be accepted",[76] and requested the Rwandan representatives present to undertake the closure of the station. The Rwandan interim government Ambassador to the UN, Jean-Damascene Bizimana, insisted "it was an independent radio station", but agreed to co-operate.[77] The Nigerian Ambassador to the UN, Ibrahim Gambari, noted:

The Security Council is extremely angry that these broadcasts by RTLM are inciting ethnic hatred and hostilities and inciting people against UNAMIR forces. ... If the interim government is indeed an interim government ... it should put a stop to this within the next 24 hours.

When asked about the promise of the Rwandan Ambassador to the UN to close RTLM, however, Ibrahim Gambari admitted, "I don't think they were serious".[78]

Notes

[1] J-P Ceppi, *Le Nouveau Quotidien*, 10 Aug. 1994, 4.

[2] A Zaka, "Les Présidents du Rwanda et du Burundi ont trouvé la mort dans le crash de leur avion", Agence France-Presse, 7 April 1994.

[3] For a discussion of theories about the plane crash, see F Reyntjens, *Rwanda: Trois jours qui ont fait basculer l'histoire (Cahiers Africains, N. 16)*, (Brussels and Paris: Institut Africain-CEDAF and l'Harmattan, 1995).

[4] "Ainsi donc Nzamurambaho nous ne savons pas ce qu'il est de lui ... le ministère de l'enseignement primaire et secondaire ... sera dirigé par Monsieur Rwamakuba André. ... je ne sais pas où Jean-Marie Vianney [Mbonimpa] se serait lui aussi ... je n'en sais rien comment cela s'est passé. ... [Valérie Bemeriki holds back from laughing and Noël Hitimana begins to giggle] Nous ne le savons pas bien [Bemeriki laughs as she speaks]. ... Nous ne le savons pas bien, mais peut-être ... nous le saurons. ... mais maintenant nous ne le savons pas. ... Ainsi nous ne savons pas Lando [Landoald Ndasingwa, Minister of Labour and Social Affairs] quant à lui ... peut-être qu'"ils" ont démissionné. ..."

[5] Reyntjens, note 3 above, at 69-74. The five Ghanaian UNAMIR troops present were also disarmed and taken to a camp but were later released.

[6] RTLM, 17 June 1994, as cited in J-P Chrétien, *Rwanda: Les médias du génocide* (Paris: Éditions Karthala, 1995), 331.

[7] "... Ils tuent cruellement l'homme ... ils le tuent en le disséquant ... en extrayant de son corps certains organes ... en lui prenant par exemple le coeur, le foie, l'estomac. ... les *inyenzi-inkotanyi* mangent les hommes". RTLM, 14 June 1994, as quoted in ibid., at 162.

[8] "Vous comprenez donc que la cruauté des *Inyenzi* est irréversible, *la cruauté des Inyenzi ne peut être guérie que par leur totale extermination*" (italics added). As quoted in ibid., at 204.

[9] "La famille en voie d'extinction au Rwanda". RTLM, 13 May 1994, as cited in ibid., at 205.

[10] "Mais donc! ces gens vont-ils continuer à se suicider ... à engager une bataille suicidaire contre un groupe nombreux ... ne vont-ils pas vraiment être exterminés?" Ibid.

[11] "Kagame n'avait pas prévu que les complices, hommes et femmes, allaient disparaître sous la poussée des citoyens, à Kigali. ... les fosses qui avaient été creusées pour les Hutu ont été utilisées pour les complices". As quoted in ibid., at 266.

[12] "Ces Tutsi ont causé l'extermination de leurs congénères... l'extermination de leurs congénères innocents ... à cause de la colère. ... suite aux attaques non fondées des *Inkotanyi*". As cited in ibid., at 197.

[13] Jean Barahinyura, leading CDR founder, interviewed by Gaspard Gahigi. "Si vous ne voulez pas faire exterminer les Rwandais, levez-vous, agissez ... sans vous soucier de l'opinion internationale. ...". Ibid., at 194.

[14] He held this position from July 1994, when the RPF took power, until late August 1995, when he was dismissed in a cabinet reshuffle.

[15] "Les citoyens sont donc priés de rester les yeux ouverts, de tenir comme de vrais hommes, pour se défendre vraiment. Les barrières doivent être maintenues. Elles doivent être maintenues vraiment pendant la journée, pour qu'ils puissent arrêter ces *Inkotanyi*. Parce qu'il y en a qui sont en train de descendre, habillés en civil et sans armes ... pour paraît-il chercher du renfort. Mais vraiment les citoyens, il faut qu'ils restent sur leurs barrières, vraiment qu'ils se défendent, qu'ils restent inébranlables vraiment".

[16] "Qu'ils [les citoyens] restent et se battent contre eux et qu'ils les terrassent vraiment. ... il faut vraiment que vous vous accrochiez, que vous combattiez ces ennemis, ravagez-les vraiment, bref défendez-vous".

[17] The expression "son of cultivator" implies "Hutu", and was coined by the singer and RTLM shareholder Simon Bikindi. His songs about "Hutu unity" reportedly were played constantly by RTLM during the genocide, sometimes up to 15 times a day.

[18] RTLM, Human Rights Watch, translated into English, 15-30 May 1994, unpublished.

[19] Human Rights Watch/Africa, *Genocide in Rwanda: April-May 1994* (New

York: May 1994), 3.

[20] "Tous ceux qui nous écoutez, continuez votre héroïsme, continuez à être héroïques, je pense que personne n'a décidé de fuir. ..."

[21] "Combattez-les avec les armes à votre disposition, vous avez des flèches, vous avez des lances. ... Prenez vos 'outils' traditionnels". As cited in Chrétien, note 6 above, at 304.

[22] "Qu'ils soient forts, radio RTLM est avec eux ... elle les suit tout le temps pendant qu'eux-mêmes passent le temps sur ... leurs barrières nuit et jour ... et radio RTLM c'est comme cela ... elle passe le temps à soutenir les gens qui sont les nôtres".

[23] "Bonjour chers amis auditeurs, bonjour aux forces armées rwandaises, bonjour à toute population rwandaise et une salutation particulière à ces habitants de Kigali et d'ailleurs de tout le pays qui font la ronde nocturne chaque jour". As cited in Reporters sans frontières, *Rwanda: médias de la haine ou presse démocratique? Rapport de mission 16-24 Sept. 1994* (Paris: RSF, 1994).

[24] RTLM, note 18 above.

[25] Ibid.

[26] Ibid.

[27] "L'homme doit se lever, ajuster son pagne et continuer. Parce que quand la bataille est là, elle est là. Plus moyen de faire autrement".

[28] RTLM, note 18 above.

[29] "Vous savez que quand ils fuient comme ça en désordre, même des *Inkotanyi* y trouvent l'occasion de se mêler à eux. C'est ce que nous appelons "infiltrations", et quand ils arrivent quelque part, ils se mettent à commettre des horreurs. ..."

[30] "Les *Inkotanyi* se sont répandus dans les broussailles ... ils sont en train de détaler sur les collines. ... Ils savent plonger et réapparaître!"

[31] "'On vient d'apprendre que Untel a des munitions'. C'était pour le signaler. Le lendemain, la milice était chez lui". C Lesnes, "Rwanda: l'engrenage du génocide vécu par un jeune Tutsi", *Le Monde*, 5 Aug. 1994.

[32] "Je viens d'apprendre que les gens qui sont allés chez lui ne l'ont pas trouvé. Où est-ce qu'il peut être? Continuez à fouiller le quartier". Reporters sans frontières, note 23 above.

[33] "Les petits *Inyenzi* ... même s'ils espéraient encore ... [être] des invités en

sécurité dans la cave de ce Sebera ... je vous disais que c'est là qu'ils sont en train de griller donc ... maintenant ils sont en train de flamber. ... Au fait ... il y en avait pas mal de "petits trucs" [RPA troops] ... ils s'étaient entassés là-dedans."

[34] After the genocide the skulls and remains of eight unidentified people were found in the house.

[35] *La Lettre de Reporters sans frontières*, No. 62 (Paris: Oct. 1994).

[36] "Je vous l'ai dit avec insistance, surtout à Gitarama et à Butare, que les Inkotanyi, surtout qu'ils disaient que la Préfecture de Butare, que c'est par là qu'ils allaient faire leur percée, et que c'est là qu'ils trouveraient la faille, et nous n'ignorons pas qu'ils y ont des complices de tous les côtés, *surtout que même le préfet de Butare, et je ne l'invente pas à sa place, lui-même a dit qu'il est membre du PL* [Parti Libéral] *mais que pour lui quand le FPR viendra, il deviendra un adepte du FPR. Alors s'il deviendra un adepte du FPR, c'est qu'il travaille déjà pour le FPR"* (italics added).

[37] For example, Human Rights Watch reported that hundreds of staff and patients were executed in a Butare hospital and that 21 Tutsi children were taken from an orphanage and killed. Human Rights Watch/Africa, note 19 above, at 3.

[38] "[Les Tutsi] qui allaient commettre l'irréparable étaient au nombre de 88. ... Cela a mal tourné lorsque le père Ngoga en personne a pris le fusil et a pris position près de l'église, et qu'il s'est mis à tirer sur les Hutu. ... pendant qu'ils pourchassaient ces Tutsi qui venaient les assaillir. Les gens l'ont vu. ... Il a pris sa voiture et a fui. ... Même aujourd'hui, il court encore". Chrétien, note 6 above, at 327-328.

[39] "Le père Ngoga n'est pas le seul. Et Muvara? ... Le père Ntagara peut-il expliquer aux Rwandais la raison pour laquelle les eucharistes ont été remplacées par les munitions?". Ibid., at 328.

[40] For example, 6,000 Tutsi were massacred in a church at Cyahinda; 2,800 were killed in a church in Kibungo; 4,000 were executed in Shangi Parish Church and 2,000 were massacred in Mibirizi Parish Church. (Human Rights Watch/Africa, note 19 above, at 3.)

[41] "Il [le Docteur] a dit "en ces temps que nous vivons ... s'il faut voir des gens se réfugier dans les paroisses ... et dans d'autres lieux" ... il a dit "ce n'est pas bien du tout" ... hm ... il a dit "en outre tu trouves que ces gens ... qu'ils [*RPF troops*] ont placé dans les paroisses et ailleurs. ... leur donnent des grenades et autres d'armes encore ... tout cela n'est pas bien".

[42] "Quelqu'un en qui j'ai confiance vraiment".

[43] Quoted in African Rights, *Death, Despair and Defiance*, Revised Edition (London: African Rights, 1995), 226.

[44] Ibid., at 704-707.

[45] After RTLM was shelled on 17 April, its broadcast range was limited.

[46] Interviewed by Gaspard Gahigi, RTLM. Translated into English by Human Rights Watch, see note 18 above.

[47] African Rights, *Rwanda: Not So Innocent — When Women Become Killers* (London: African Rights, 1995), 134-142.

[48] Ibid., at 9.

[49] Radio Muhabura (English), 1900 GMT, 16 April 1994, in *BBC Summary of World Broadcasts*.

[50] African Rights, note 43 above, at 80.

[51] During the genocide, he was promoted to Editor-in-Chief of Radio Rwanda. He continued to periodically file reports for the BBC until July 1994.

[52] G Prunier, *The Rwanda Crisis 1959-1994: History of a Genocide* (London and New York: Hurst & Company and Columbia University Press), 224.

[53] Radio Rwanda, Kigali (French), 1000 GMT, 12 April 1994, in *BBC Summary of World Broadcasts*, 14 April 1994.

[54] Radio Rwanda, Kigali (French), 0407 GMT, 9 April 1994, "New president addresses the nation, announces composition of new government", *BBC Summary of World Broadcasts*, 11 April 1994.

[55] Ibid.

[56] "Il y a eu des affrontements au sein de la population, surtout dans la ville de Kigali et les gens ont été tués, parmi lesquels le Premier Ministre, Madame Uwilingiyimana Agathe, et quelques ministres, ainsi que plusieurs citoyens". Chrétien, note 6 above, at 301.

[57] "C'est donc cela qui a entrainé en grande partie ces troubles, notre souhait étant que les gens essaient de le comprendre. ... que les gens comprennent les raisons qui ont provoqué des actes de violence d'une telle ampleur". Ibid.

[58] Radio Rwanda, Kigali (Kinyarwanda), 1140 GMT, 9 April 1994, "New president addresses parliament, defends decision to assume power", in *BBC Summary of World Broadcasts*, 11 April 1994.

[59] "Dix-maisons", administrative units comprising 10 houses. ARTICLE 19

believes that these were the smallest administrative divisions in Rwanda.

[60] "Le préfet de la préfecture de Kigali demande à tous les citoyens de continuer à garder l'oeil ouvert pour qu'ensemble avec l'armée du pays ils défendent l'intégrité de notre pays. Les citoyens se-sont donc unis aux gouvernants qui leur sont proches, les 'dix-maisons', les responsables de cellules, les conseillers communaux, les bourgemestres et même les responsables des partis, ils doivent se mobiliser pour la sécurité dans leurs cellules et secteurs pour qu'ils démasquent celui qui se cacherait au milieu d'eux dans l'intention de soutenir l'ennemi."

[61] "Pour cette raison ils [les citoyens] doivent surveiller tous les chemins et en outre là où ils soupçonnent que l'ennemi se cacherait, quel que soit l'endroit, qu'ils le débusquent sans modération. Les habitants sont priés de ne pas abandonner leurs maisons car ce serait donner une brèche à l'ennemi. Ils sont priés de procéder à des rondes ainsi que de suivre Radio Rwanda. ...".

[62] "... Nous tous ensemble, nous devons mener cette guerre ... c'est une guerre finale, il faut justement la finir. ... J'adresse spécialement ce message à certains bourgemestres dont on m'a rapporté qu'ils sont allés s'entraîner chez les *inkotanyi* ... qu'ils [*les bourgemestres*] leur [*the RPA troops*] fassent comprendre que le gouvernement est détérminé. L'Etat, les militaires, la population, nous nous sommes décidés à mener cette guerre et à la gagner". As cited in Chrétien, note 6 above, at 300.

[63] "Pendant ces périodes difficiles, notre souhait c'est que ces forces [de sécurité] soient épaulées; par toutes les forces vives de la population; toutes, nous tous. Que personne ne dise "moi, ça ne me regarde pas" ("je ne suis pas concerné"). ... La sécurité n'est pas une affaire de gendarmes uniquement; la sécurité est une affaire qui concerne en premier lieu la population; les gendarmes n'interviennent qu'après, quand la population rencontre des difficultés à surmonter". Translated into French by Human Rights Watch (unpublished).

[64] Ibid.

[65] As quoted in M Wrong, "Exiled Rwanda Broadcaster has no regrets", Reuters, 24 Aug. 1994.

[66] As cited by Agence France-Presse, "Hutu extremist radio reportedly broadcasts from Gisenyi", 10 July 1994.

[67] "Est-ce que un journaliste qui parle d'un problème existant réellement et qui menace une société, est-ce que le journaliste est coupable de l'avoir dit ou plutôt il serait coupable de ne l'avoir pas dit. ... Puisque tous les médias maintenant du monde entier sont unanimes pour reconnaître qu'au Rwanda, il y a un problème ethnique qui a débouché à la catastrophe humaine à laquelle

nous assistons aujourd'hui. ... Est-ce que si la RTLM ne l'avait pas dit, est-ce que ça aurait empêché ce problème d'exister?"

[68] "En disant la vérité, en disant la vraie face du FPR. ... Il a commencé à faire une propagande anti-RTLM. Et c'est comme cela que la RTLM se retrouve maintenant, ou même avant qu'on ne quitte le pays, se retrouve la bête noire du FPR".

[69] "C'est une radio privée dont le gouvernement n'a pas le contrôle". J Garrus "Appui américain", Agence France-Presse, 4 May 1994.

[70] RTBF, 16 April 1994.

[71] Ibid.

[72] As quoted in C McGreal, "Rwanda: Inside Story — Blood on their Hands," *The Guardian*, 3 Dec. 1994.

[73] Joint Evaluation of Emergency Assistance to Rwanda, *The International Response to Conflict and Genocide: Lessons from the Rwanda Experience (Study 2: Early Warning and Conflict Management)*, (Denmark: Steering Committee of the Joint Evaluation of Emergency Assistance to Rwanda, March 1996), 55.

[74] H Deguine, *Le Monde Diplomatique*, March 1995.

[75] As quoted on Radio France Internationale, "French to prevent broadcasts from safe zone calling on Rwandans to leave", 21 July 1994.

[76] F Haq, "Rwanda: Close down Anti-Tutsi Radio, Says UN Security Council," Inter-Press Service, 27 June 1994.

[77] Ibid.

[78] Ibid.

INTERNATIONAL LAW, THE MEDIA AND GENOCIDE

There are a number of sources of international law relating to propaganda and incitement to genocide and communal hatred. The Genocide Convention defines several offences pertaining to the crime of genocide under which individuals may be prosecuted. International human rights treaties impose various obligations on governments to prevent and prohibit propaganda for war and incitement to discrimination or hatred.

1   The Genocide Convention

The Convention on the Prevention and Punishment of the Crime of Genocide obliges states parties to enact laws to ensure the prosecution of and effective penalties for any persons found guilty of genocide or any of the other related crimes that the Convention declares shall be punished, including "direct and public incitement to commit genocide"; "attempt to commit genocide"; and "complicity in genocide".[1] Genocide is defined as: "any of the following acts committed with intent to destroy, in whole or in part, a national, ethnical, racial or religious group, as such: (a) killing members of the group; (b) causing serious bodily or mental harm to members of the group; (c) deliberately inflicting on the group conditions of life calculated to bring about its physical destruction in whole or in part ...".[2] The Convention specifies that *any* persons who commit genocide or a related crime "shall be punished" regardless of "whether they are constitutionally responsible rulers, public officials or private individuals". Furthermore, the Convention requires states parties either to ensure that such persons are "tried by a competent tribunal" in the territory where the act was committed or else "by such international penal tribunal as may have jurisdiction".[3]

The most important case law in this regard derives from the International Military Tribunal at Nuremberg, which tried the perpetrators of the Nazi genocide of European Jews. Among those prosecuted was Julius Streicher, the publisher of *Der Stürmer*, a weekly anti-Semitic newspaper. He wrote and published articles that called for the annihilation of the Jews. The Tribunal found that Streicher was not sufficiently closely connected with Hitler's inner circle or the formulation of policies that led to war to be found guilty of crimes against peace (the first count of the Nuremberg indictment). However it did find him guilty of count four, crimes against humanity:

> Streicher's incitement to murder and extermination at the time when Jews in the East were being killed under the most horrible conditions clearly constitutes persecution on political and racial grounds in connection with War Crimes, as defined by the Charter [of the Tribunal], and constitutes a Crime against Humanity.

In contrast, Hans Fritsche, head of the Radio Division of the Reich Ministry of Propaganda and Enlightenment was acquitted. The Tribunal found that he had used the media "to arouse popular sentiment in support of Hitler and the German war effort" rather than to incite the Germans to commit atrocities. It also 'concluded that he was mainly a "conduit" who followed instructions that came from the Minister, Josef Goebbels, and thus was not responsible even if the propaganda he relayed resulted in atrocities. This second part of the holding has been considered controversial and probably would be rejected by any international court today.

2   The State's Obligations to Stop Incitement to Violence

Two international human rights treaties in particular require governments to take concrete measures against violence and incitement to violence based on ethnic hatred: the International Convention on the Elimination of All Forms of Racial Discrimination (ICERD) and the International Covenant on Civil and Political Rights (ICCPR).

Article 20(2) of the ICCPR imposes on states parties the obligation to "prohibit by law ... [a]ny advocacy of national, racial or religious hatred that constitutes incitement to discrimination, hostility or violence".[4] ICERD imposes a similar and arguably even stronger obligation.[5] These treaties clearly apply to hatred and violence between Tutsi and Hutu: "racial discrimination" is defined to include any distinction based on "race, colour, descent, or national or ethnic origin which has the purpose or effect of nullifying or impairing the ... exercise, on an equal footing, of human rights and fundamental freedoms ...".[6] These treaties are to be interpreted and applied "with due regard to the principles embodied in the Universal Declaration of Human Rights and the rights expressly [enumerated]", including the right to freedom of expression.[7]

These provisions impose three main obligations on governments. First and foremost, governments must ensure that no public institutions or authorities participate in any way in any of the enumerated crimes of incitement.[8] Where the state controls broadcasting, it has a direct legal responsibility to ensure that the state-run media do not incite violence or hatred.[9] Second, governments must adopt laws that make incitement to violence a crime.[10] Third, governments must investigate complaints of violations and pursue prosecution and punishment where evidence of these crimes is established.[11]

The obligation to investigate and prosecute is strongest where evidence suggests that public institutions or authorities are either directly or indirectly involved in inciting violence; in such cases, where the evidence of a crime is sufficient, prosecution or, at the very least, some effective corrective action, is mandatory.[12]

A government's obligation to prosecute private media or individuals is less strong; the obligation is discretionary, but it is likely that a government will be found to have abused its discretion if it fails to take action to investigate and remedy (though not necessarily prosecute) clear-cut violations, unless there is a very compelling governmental interest counselling against investigation.[13]

The burden of imposing restrictions on freedom of expression always rests with the party seeking to impose or justify the restrictions.[14] The burden is all the greater where the government seeks to impose a restriction that will substantially diminish the free flow of information from a variety of sources.[15]

ARTICLE 19 is not unmindful of arguments that efforts to prosecute high-ranking government authorities or people with close ties to the government or military could destabilize the government. This argument has been made with particular force regarding nominally democratic governments that succeed criminally abusive regimes, but it also applies to weak governments that are trying to stave off civil war. ARTICLE 19 notes that international law itself allows a measure of flexibility to governments that face exceptional circumstances. The value of international legal norms is that, forged as they are through the experience and practice of governments including when faced with threats to their very existence, they provide some means by which to limit the ability of governments to abuse their discretion with impunity.[16]

3 The State's Obligation to Disseminate, and Promote the Dissemination of, Accurate and Balanced Information

The rights to freedom of expression and information have been recognized as essential pillars of democratic society by institutions and governments around the world. The UN General Assembly, at its first session, declared: "Freedom of information is a fundamental human right and ... the touchstone of all of the freedoms to which the United Nations is consecrated".[17] The European Court of Human Rights has repeatedly affirmed that "Freedom of expression constitutes one of the essential foundations of such [democratic] society, one of the basic conditions for its progress and for the development of every man". The need to safeguard these rights is all the more crucial where democracy is under threat or is struggling to claim a toe-hold.

In most circumstances, the communications media are the main vehicles for promoting freedom of expression and information, and the government's role is to refrain from interfering with the private media, to grant full editorial independence to the public media, and to promote media pluralism, including by encouraging a diversity of sources of information.

However, in a situation, such as Rwanda in the early 1990s and Burundi today, where there are few media organs that are independent of the government or political parties, the government is obliged to ensure that state-run media fulfil the principal function of the private media, namely to impart information and ideas of public interest. Moreover, the government is obliged to impart information that is both accurate and balanced, and to strive to promote tolerance and reduce violence. These obligations derive directly from the fundamental rights of the public to access to information necessary to protect their life and health, to non-discrimination, and to security and physical integrity.

4 Circumstances in which the International Community May Intervene to Suppress Incitement to Violence

A national government is entitled to close down or jam a radio station on the grounds that it threatens public order and, indeed, the security of the government.[18] However, the lawfulness of any assistance from the international community in furtherance of this objective is shaky at best. A government is entitled to seek support from other governments, and other governments are entitled to provide support, to assist in quelling an armed uprising unless the uprising is consistent with the UN Charter. Armed rebellions may be consistent with the Charter if, for example, they are in pursuit of a legitimate claim of self-determination or they represent a "recourse [of] last resort to rebellion against tyranny and oppression".[19] If a rebellion reaches that stage, and attracts widespread popular support or attains control over significant areas of the country, outside assistance to either side is widely viewed by international experts as an intervention in violation of the UN Charter in the internal affairs of a country.[20]

The international community may intervene to jam broadcasts where violence is already under way and there is clear evidence that the broadcasts could incite genocide, crimes against humanity or violence on such a scale as to threaten international peace and security.[21] International peace and security is understood to be threatened by the creation of massive refugee flows across international borders, especially in an area that is already unable to cope with the huge numbers of displaced people.

Notes

[1] *The Convention on the Prevention and Punishment of the Crime of Genocide,* approved and opened for signature by UN General Assembly resolution 260A (III) on 9 Dec. 1948; entered into force on 12 Jan. 1951, Art. III(c), (d) and (e).

[2] Art. II.

[3] Art. IV.

[4] The Human Rights Committee has interpreted Art. 20(2) to require states parties to provide for an "appropriate sanction in case of violation". General Comment No. 11(19), 1983 *Annual Report of the Human Rights Committee,* UN Doc. A/38/40, Annex VI (1983). This has been interpreted to mean that sanctions other than criminal punishments are permissible for less serious infractions.

[5] Art. 4(a) requires states parties to declare to be a crime "all dissemination of ideas based on racial superiority or hatred, incitement to racial discrimination, as well as all acts of violence or incitement to such acts against any race or persons of another colour or ethnic origin ..."

[6] ICERD, Art. 1(1). Even if a distinction between Tutsi and Hutu based on ethnicity were to be disputed, there is no dispute that a distinction exists based on descent.

[7] For a fuller discussion of the requisite balancing, see K J Partsch, "Racial Speech and Human Rights," in S Coliver (ed., for ARTICLE 19), *Striking a Balance: Hate Speech, Freedom of Expression and Non-discrimination* (London: ARTICLE 19 and the University of Essex, 1993), 23-25.

[8] CERD, Art. 2(1)a and b, and ICCPR, Art. 2(1).

[9] F Hampson, "Incitement and the Media: Responsibility of and for the Media in the Conflicts in the Former Yugoslavia" *Papers in the Theory and Practice of Human Rights,* Number 3 (Colchester, UK: Human Rights Centre, University of Essex, 1993), 4.

[10] ICCPR, Art. 2(2) and CERD, Art. 2(1)c and d.

[11] *Velasquez Rodriguez v. Honduras*, Inter-American Court of Human Rights, Judgment of 29 July 1988, Series C no. 4, at paras. 166, 172; *Artze fur das Leben v. Austria*, Judgment of 21 June 1988, Series A no. 139, at para. 34.

[12] *Velasquez Rodriguez v. Honduras*, note 11 above, at paras. 172-174.

[13] E.g., *L K v. the Netherlands*, CERD, Communication No. 4/1991. In this case, the Committee that monitors compliance with ICERD concluded that the municipal government of Utrecht violated the treaty when it failed to take any action in response to a complaint filed by a Moroccan citizen that he had been subjected to clear-cut racist remarks.

[14] ARTICLE 19, *The ARTICLE 19 Freedom of Expression Handbook* (London: ARTICLE 19, 1993), 109-113, and authorities cited thereat.

[15] See, e.g., European Court of Human Rights, *Informationsverein Lentia and Others v. Austria,* Judgment of 24 Nov. 1993, Series A no. 276, para. 38 ("the State is the ultimate guarantor" of the principle of media pluralism which is necessary if the media are to accomplish their public tasks of informing the public and serving as a watchdog of government).

[16] See generally, D Orentlicher, "Settling Accounts: The Duty to Prosecute Human Rights Violations of A Prior Regime," in 100 *Yale L. Journal* (1993), 2540 *et seq.*

[17] G.A. Resolution 59(I), 14 Dec. 1946.

[18] Art. 19 of the ICCPR authorizes governments to impose restrictions on freedom of expression so long as such restrictions are prescribed by law and are necessary to protect one of the enumerated interests, which include "the protection of national security or ... public order".

[19] UDHR, preamble, para. 3. As stated by the UN Human Rights Committee in its General Comment on Art. 20 of the ICCPR, "The provisions of article 20 ... do not prohibit advocacy of the sovereign right of self-defence or the right of peoples to self-determination and independence in accordance with the Charter of the United Nations". General Comment 11 on Art. 20 (1983), para. 2, reprinted in "Compilation of General Comments and General Recommendations Adopted by Human Rights Treaty Bodies", UN Doc. HRI/GEN/1/Rev.1, of 29 July 1994.

[20] As stated by Oscar Schachter, a leading US authority on the subject: "Such outside support would be contrary to the right of the people to decide the issue by their own means. It would be immaterial whether the insurgency was directed at overthrow of the government or at secession (or autonomy) of a territorial unit". O Schachter, "The Right of States to Use Armed Force", in L Henkin, R Pugh, O Schachter and H Smit, *International Law: Cases and*

Materials (2nd edn), (Minnesota: West Publishing Co., 1987), 758.

[21] Hampson, note 9 above, at 15.

CONCLUSION

In communal conflicts and humanitarian disasters the mass media have enormous power for good or evil. The very language used can influence the perception of where responsibility for conflict lies. For example, when the South African media reported on "black on black" violence in the townships and squatter camps of KwaZulu-Natal they fuelled the view that violence was somehow the natural condition of African society and that blacks were unready for democratic power. In reality, of course, the violence was largely provoked by state-sponsored hit squads and militias. Similarly, in the Rift Valley of Kenya the use of the term "tribal clashes" has obscured the fact that political violence has been organized by the government to drive opposition supporters from the province.

Nevertheless, whether this power is as great as the media themselves would like to believe is a moot point. To some extent, discussion of the role of RTLM in Rwanda's genocide has been influenced by the international media's fascination with the potential impact of their own technology.

The international media's continued emphasis on the role played by RTLM distracts attention from its failure to report and analyze the causes of the genocide adequately as it occurred. The Joint Evaluation of Emergency Assistance to Rwanda concluded that "Inadequate and inaccurate reporting by international media on the genocide itself contributed to international indifference and inaction".[1] For example,

> US television coverage and CNN erred on the side of vagueness, generally referring to "unspeakable atrocities", and "ethnic violence", but picked up the theme of tribal or mutual ethnic slaughter. It would not be until 7 May that ABC correspondent Ron Allen suggested that the events were not a product of spontaneous tribal violence, but were a premeditated political act intended as a final solution.[2]

161

According to the Evaluation, the international media chose not to report on evidence of plans for the genocide. However, the Evaluation also acknowledged that media coverage during the genocide "influenced [humanitarian] agencies to act urgently and responsibly, and raised awareness of politicians and the public at large".[3]

However, the inaction of the international community in response to the threat of genocide was a failure not of the media, but of international institutions, which did not react to information which was readily available to them. The media have no obligation, beyond their own professional standards, to report adequately on human rights issues. The institutions of the UN and the Organization of African Unity, as well as their member states, do have legal obligations under their founding charters and a variety of treaties.

The failure of the international community to intervene in time to prevent the Rwandan genocide is often described as a failure of early warning. This is extremely misleading, since it carries the implication that if only the higher echelons of the UN system and Western governments had known of the impending genocide, then they would have taken action. Yet the Rwandan genocide was very clearly signposted. The international community received three explicit warnings in particular, two of them from within the UN system.

Firstly, in March 1993 an International Commission of Investigation composed of representatives of four non-governmental human rights groups reported on political violence and other human rights violations from October 1990. The report documented the establishment of the death squads of "Network Zero" and the *Interahamwe* and *Impuzamugambi* militias, as well as their links to government. It pointed out the role of Radio Rwanda in broadcasting propaganda for violence and documented explicitly genocidal statements such as the November 1992 speech by Léon Mugesera. The report concluded:

> Testimony established that many Rwandans have been killed for the sole reason that they were Tutsi. The question remains whether the designation of some members of the Tutsi ethnic group as a target for destruction demonstrates an intention, in the sense of the [Genocide] Convention, to destroy this

group or a part of it because of its members' ethnicity.[4]

Secondly, in his report of 11 August 1993, the UN Special Rapporteur on Extradjudicial, Summary or Arbitrary Executions, Bacre Waly Ndiaye, described death threats and political assassinations against government opponents. He noted:

> A study of the phases preceding outbreaks of violence among the population shows that such outbreaks were planned and prepared, with targets being identified in speeches by representatives of the authorities, broadcasts on Rwandese radio and leaflets.[5]

Like the International Commission of Investigation, the Special Rapporteur raised the prospect of genocide.

Thirdly, in January 1994, the commander of the UN peacekeeping mission in Rwanda, General Romeo Dallaire, reported to the UN Secretariat in New York that his intelligence network had gathered details of plans for genocide, including the training of militias, caching of arms and lists of victims. The Secretariat questioned the accuracy of the intelligence and made no contingency plans to deal with genocide.[6]

To explain this failure is more difficult. Despite the general perception that the UN in the post-Cold War era is better able to deal with humanitarian crises, the fact remains that it is still dependent on the political will of its most powerful member states. The United States had been badly burned by the failure of the UNOSOM operation in Somalia, while all the major powers were deeply preoccupied with the crisis in former Yugoslavia. The only major power with a strong interest in the region, France, was an active supporter of the Habyarimana regime. Even those governments which evinced a clear concern about the human rights situation in Rwanda, such as Belgium and Canada, were reluctant to attach full human rights conditions to their aid because they wanted to be seen to support democratization and the Arusha peace process.

163

The Joint Evaluation of Emergency Assistance to Rwanda has fully documented these failures. It poses the question of whether aid conditionality and an arms embargo between 1990 and 1993 would have defused the conflict and prevented genocide. Ultimately such speculations can never be conclusive. However the Joint Evaluation report observes that "firmer conclusions can be drawn about what did happen":

> By not standing firm on human rights conditionality, donors collectively sent the message that their priorities lay elsewhere. By permitting arms to reach the Rwandese protagonists, the possibilities for demilitarizing the conflict were reduced. Arms supplies reinforced the determination of both parties to seek a military and forceful solution to a political conflict.[7]

The broadcasts of Radio Rwanda were an extremely important source of early warning – one which was utilized by both the International Commission of Investigation and Special Rapporteur Bacre Waly Ndiaye. The latter stated in his August 1993 report that incitement to racial hatred had been noted on several occasions, for example through Radio Rwanda.[8] The content of news programmes in the Rwandan media differed substantially depending on whether the listener was receiving the French version or the version in Kinyarwanda.[9]

In his recommendations the Special Rapporteur suggested that a radio link be set up in order to inform the population about the violence which had taken place. The aim of this would be to stop delays in information as well as failures and manipulation of communication.[10] He also suggested that a national reconciliation campaign should be organized in order to stop the "incitement to hatred". The campaign should begin with a public commitment to reconciliation on the part of the authorities, broadcast in both French and Kinyarwanda and it should be followed by a series of public education programmes about human rights.[11]

Finally, Mr Ndiaye suggested that media-related action should take place in order to prevent future incitement to hatred by the media.

Conclusion

A reform of the role and structure of the media should be envisaged. Journalists have already begun to study this question and have adopted a code of ethics. They should be provided with training opportunities, in order to enhance their professionalism and eliminate any lingering partisan tendencies. The Minister for Information is also attempting to effect reforms, but his powers are limited and his action too often thwarted.[12]

Subsequent commentary has drawn a much more radical conclusion: that "hate media" should be banned. This lesson has been applied first in relation to Burundi. This is always seen as Rwanda's "twin", since it shares an almost identical ethnic make-up, although the political balance of forces is quite different. Some freedom of expression activists, including the French organization *Reporters sans frontières*, have explicitly called for bans on extremist media. In March 1996, the Burundian government responded by proscribing seven newspapers. While it is clear that international law would permit such bans and proscriptions in certain circumstances, they should be treated with great caution, for two principal reasons.

Firstly, the authorities which implement bans are not themselves impartial. In part, this is connected with the danger of applying the lessons of Rwanda mechanically to its neighbour. Whereas in Rwanda the hate media were linked formally or informally to the government, in Burundi they are attached to various political factions. There is thus little chance that a ban will be enforced impartially.

Secondly, the emphasis on the media always tends to distract attention from the root of the problem, which is the formal and informal structures, both political and military, which plan and carry out human rights abuses, up to and including genocide. Thus the UN Human Rights Commission, meeting in Geneva in April 1996, passed a resolution condemning hate media in Burundi in preference to a stronger resolution addressing the various political actors. Similarly, the previous month, the UN Security Council requested "Member States and others to cooperate in the identification and dismantling of radio stations which incite hatred and acts of violence in Burundi".[13]

The fundamental reality, which cannot be stated too often, is that genocide is not caused by the mass media. At worst they may abet the process, but inflammatory media coverage is essentially a symptom of a process resulting from other causes. ARTICLE 19 endorses the approach taken by Bacre Waly Ndiaye, which was to use the hate broadcasts of Radio Rwanda as an early warning of impending genocide and to try to curb the impact of such broadcasts by extending media pluralism.

The alternative notion that the media caused the genocide in Rwanda — that it would not have taken place without RTLM — rests upon a specific interpretation of the genocide which was prevalent in the international media at the time but which does not stand up to serious scrutiny. This is the interpretation which sees the genocide as the expression of primordial blood-lust between the Hutu and Tutsi communities which only requires inflammatory propaganda to provoke outright violence. Yet all the evidence points to the fact that the Rwandan genocide was a highly planned affair in which the initial targets were moderate politicians from both communities. The apparatus of militias, hit squads, arms caches and death lists was meticulously put in place in the months before April 1994 — as documented by the UN military mission in Rwanda and ignored by the UN Secretariat.

Much subsequent commentary on the role of RTLM has tended to conflate the station's broadcasts before and during the genocide. For example, a study commissioned by UNESCO (United Nations Educational, Scientific and Cultural Organization) quotes only from broadcasts after 6 April 1994, although it purports to describe the nature of RTLM's pre-genocide propaganda as well.[14] Yet, as the present report has demonstrated, RTLM's broadcasts before and after 6 April were significantly different.

In ARTICLE 19's view the issue of RTLM's post-6 April broadcasts is a relatively simple one which does not greatly bear upon conventional debates about "hate speech" and freedom of expression. The term "incitement to genocide" is inadequate to describe the role of RTLM once the killing was under way. The radio station did not incite genocide so much as organize it, notably by identifying targets, broadcasting vehicle number-plates, refuges where potential victims were hiding and so on. ARTICLE 19 does not consider that there is a freedom of expression issue involved here: giving orders to carry out human rights abuses is not protected whether this is done in writing, orally, by two-way radio or by public broadcast. International law clearly permitted external intervention to jam the broadcasts at this stage, which is the course of action which should have been undertaken.

The question of what action should have been taken to counteract inflammatory propaganda on RTLM and Radio Rwanda *before* the genocide is altogether more complex. Radio Rwanda was formally a government radio station, while RTLM was one in practice. This makes the issue rather different from the usual debate about "hate speech" which tends to focus on private individuals. However, it also means that there was a set of other standards which could have been invoked to require the authorities to cease broadcasting ethnic propaganda. Thus the focus could have been on promoting Article 19 of the International Covenant on Civil and Political Rights (ICCPR) — a positive obligation to promote freedom of expression and plurality — rather than solely on Article 20 which restricts incitement to hatred.

ARTICLE 19's view is that it would not have been correct to call for a ban on hate media such as RTLM in the months before the genocide, a lesson which applies in contemporary Burundi. The emphasis should rather be on promoting pluralism in privately-owned media and supporting attempted reform of the state broadcasting system as a means of marginalizing extremist propaganda and developing the middle ground. It might be objected that this would have been a hopelessly idealistic and impractical position to take in the weeks immediately before April 1994. However, the alternative position — to call upon the Rwandan government or judiciary to close down RTLM — was also entirely unrealistic and any call for international action to jam the broadcasts would not have been sanctioned by law. If useful lessons are to be drawn from the Rwandan situation it is necessary to go back to the introduction of multi-party politics and the failure to build adequate institutional support for democracy.

In one sense the Rwandan experience is not atypical. In countries like Kenya and Zambia, which also underwent rapid democratic transitions under pressure from Western donor governments, there has also been a failure to transform or replace the institutions of one-party rule in order to make them more accessible and accountable. In particular the mass media have changed very little. Broadcasting remains a virtual state monopoly, while the independent press exists in an almost permanent state of siege. Even countries which democratized later and constructed better constitutional safeguards — Malawi is a good example — nevertheless have failed to establish an independent and accountable publicly-funded state broadcasting system.

In 1990 none of the external forces with influence over the Habyarimana government attached much importance to the role of the mass media in democratization. In reality, participation in multi-party politics means very little if the mass of the population has no access to information and little opportunity to express its views. In this respect Rwanda differed little from Kenya, Zambia, Malawi or any one of a number of African transitional democracies. The implications were more explosive in Rwanda because without open debate about policy issues, politics tended to revert to expressions of the interests of Hutu or Tutsi. In fact, the countervailing tendencies were quite strong in both Rwanda and Burundi. In Rwanda the moderate centre ground was strong and popular. Although the inclusion of main opposition parties in a succession of transitional governments was a major step forward in representing the moderate centre, channels for popular debate within the mass media remained dominated by the MRND.

Two important institutional changes were required in 1990. Firstly, the publicly funded broadcaster, Radio Rwanda, should have been detached from the government, with an independently-appointed board of management, financial autonomy and full editorial independence. Secondly, an independent and accountable system should have been established to oversee the licensing and regulation of independent broadcasting. Licences should have been granted according to pre-established and publicly available criteria, which would include consideration of the balance of political and ethnic viewpoints across the broadcasting spectrum. Such a system, properly enforced, would probably have precluded the licensing of a station such as RTLM.

The best means of broadcasting regulation is to have a single independent licensing authority responsible for both public and privately-funded broadcasting. This has the effect of putting an extra buffer between government and the public broadcaster, as well as ensuring that both broadcasting sectors are answerable to the same standards. Such an independent authority would contain a mechanism for considering complaints from the public about the broadcast media and imposing sanctions against broadcasters who fail to honour the terms of their licences. Alone among newly democratized African countries, South Africa has introduced such a system. This has effectively guaranteed both an independent and critical public broadcaster, the South African Broadcasting Corporation, and a vibrant and pluralistic commercial and community broadcasting sector.

It is important to understand that although the outcome of the Rwandan tragedy was extreme and exceptional, its earlier course was not at all unusual. Rwanda's imperfect democratization and failure to carry out institutional reform was, as we have argued, typical of transitional democracies in the region. Similarly the broadcasts of Radio Rwanda in 1990 and 1991 were typical of state-controlled media in a situation where national security is perceived to be threatened. They were shrill, inaccurate and ethnically biased, simultaneously exaggerating both the extent of the security threat posed by the RPF and the military successes of the Rwandan armed forces. Anti-RPF propaganda was consistently used to score political points against the non-violent parties participating in the democratization process. However, if one considered, for example, the broadcasts of the Zimbabwe Broadcasting Corporation at the height of the Matabeleland crisis in the mid-1980s, one would find precisely the same mixture.

It is argued that the difference in Rwanda was that Radio Rwanda, and later RTLM, played upon deep-rooted ethnic fears to create a situation in which radical measures — genocide — were seen to be the only solution. This is undoubtedly true, yet what was surely required was that such communal fears be confronted not suppressed. That is why the main emphasis of freedom of expression advocates in such situations must be on encouraging a plurality of viewpoints rather than suppressing the obnoxious ones. Those who call for the banning of some radio broadcasts run the risk of playing into the hands of governments which seek to restrict freedom of expression. A common refrain among governments that have democratized reluctantly is to argue that ethnic strife is caused by "too much" democracy — that single-party systems are better at fostering national unity. In reality, ethnic conflict has often been caused by deliberate manipulation on the part of the authorities, combined with an absence of any public awareness of issues of policy.

An accountable system of broadcasting regulation should, in any event, have provided the means for preventing the broadcasting of propaganda for genocide over the airwaves. The debate about RTLM has largely been posed in terms of whether the station should have been banned or its broadcasts jammed. In practice, there are a series of other measures which could be taken either by a regulatory authority or through the judicial system. These range from a formal warning, to criminal prosecution for incitement to violence (if the evidence for such a charge exists), to withdrawal of a broadcasting licence.

Of course, such discussion sounds like day-dreaming in the context of immediate pre-genocide Rwanda. RTLM was closely linked to MRND figures within the government and was an integral part of the plans for genocide. There was no independent regulatory authority for broadcasting — nor even an independent judiciary. The political conditions for regulating hate broadcasting did not exist. However, the conclusion to be drawn from this is precisely that the international community needed urgently to address the rise in violence by the MRND and CDR militias and the plans for genocide. This was not primarily a media issue. The genocide would have gone ahead with or without RTLM.

However, if the Rwandan lesson is to be of relevance to those concerned with the media and freedom of expression, it is essential to address these questions from an earlier point — from the moment of democratic transition and the need for institution-building. Nowhere is likely to suffer a Rwanda-style genocide — not even Burundi. However, many countries in the region are vulnerable to the instability caused by state-sponsored ethnic propaganda and the organization of "privatized" or informal repression by ethnic militias or private armies. The example of the state-sponsored attacks by Kalenjin "warriors" in the Kenyan Rift Valley or Inkatha *impis* in South Africa show that this problem is not unique to Rwanda. Hence the urgency of freeing broadcasting systems from government control so that their propaganda cannot be used to reinforce ethnic division.

Conclusion

Summary of conclusions and recommendations

•   The owners and broadcasters of RTLM should be indicted for crimes of genocide before the International Criminal Tribunal for Rwanda. These charges should relate to the role played by RTLM in directing the genocide from 6 April 1994 onwards. It is not recommended that charges be brought in relation to the propaganda role of RTLM or Radio Rwanda before 6 April.

•   Governments in the region, including those of Rwanda and Burundi, should reform broadcasting to ensure that the publicly funded broadcaster is institutionally, financially and editorially independent of government and that there is an independent and transparent system for the fair allocation of broadcasting licences. The licensing authority should have a complaints procedure and the power to impose sanctions on broadcasters violating the terms of their licence, up to and including withdrawal of the licence.

•   Governments in the region, with external assistance as necessary, should seek to strengthen the judiciary to ensure that the necessary steps can be taken within the domestic legal system to prevent the broadcasting of incitement to violence.

•   Governments should ratify the relevant international treaties prohibiting incitement to violence, discrimination and genocide, notably the International Covenant on Civil and Political Rights (ICCPR) and the Genocide Convention. They should take any necessary steps to incorporate these provisions into national law.

•   The international community should monitor "hate radio", particularly when linked to government authorities, and restrictions on freedom of expression as an early warning of potential gross violations of human rights. This will require a greater responsiveness on the part of the UN Secretariat to warnings generated through other parts of the UN apparatus, notably the special mechanisms dealing with human rights.

• In situations of potential communal conflict, the international community should encourage radio stations and other media which promote tolerance and a variety of viewpoints, whether these broadcast from within the country or from outside in vernacular languages. International bodies should strengthen their programmes of professional training for journalists in countries affected or endangered by communal conflict.

• The main reforms needed to prevent genocide or other gross abuses of human rights lie outside the sphere of the media. They include: reform of the security forces to make them impartial and accountable; ending the culture of impunity by holding perpetrators to account for human rights violations; establishing an independent and impartial judiciary; developing a culture and institutions of popular democratic participation. The media can assist in this process by exposing wrongdoing by state agents — in particular covert manipulation of ethnic grievances by government agents.

Notes

[1] Joint Evaluation of Emergency Assistance to Rwanda, *The International Response to Conflict and Genocide: Lessons from the Rwanda Experience, (Synthesis Report)* (Denmark: Steering Committee of the Joint Evaluation of Emergency Assistance to Rwanda, March 1996), 66.

[2] Joint Evaluation of Emergency Assistance to Rwanda, *The International Response to Conflict and Genocide: Lessons from the Rwanda Experience, (Study 1: Historical Perspective: Some Explanatory Factors)* (Denmark: Steering Committee of the Joint Evaluation of Emergency Assistance to Rwanda, March 1996), 47.

[3] Joint Evaluation of Emergency Assistance to Rwanda, note 1 above, at 66.

[4] Fédération internationale des droits de l'homme, Africa Watch, Union interafricaine des droits de l'homme et des peuples, Centre international des droits de la personne et du développement démocratique, *Report of the International Commission of Investigation on Human Rights Violations in Rwanda Since October 1, 1990 (January 7-21, 1993) Final Report* (New York: Human Rights Watch/Africa, March 1993), 29.

[5] UN Doc. E/CN.4/1994/7/Add.1, 11 Aug. 1993, para. 42.

Conclusion

[6] Joint Evaluation of Emergency Assistance to Rwanda, note 1 above, at 19.

[7] Ibid., at 18.

[8] The visit on which the report was based took place before RTLM was established.

[9] UN Economic and Social Council, *Extrajudicial, Summary or Arbitrary Executions, Addendum – Report by Mr B W Ndiaye, Special Rapporteur, on his mission to Rwanda from 8 to 17 April 1993*, UN Doc. E/CN.4/1994/7/Add. 1., dated 11 Aug. 1993, para. 56-58.

[10] Ibid., para. 65.

[11] Ibid., para. 68.

[12] Ibid., para. 69.

[13] UN Security Council Resolution 1049 (1996), UN Doc. S/RES/1049 (1996), 5 Mar. 1996. para. 5, at 2.

[14] J-P Chrétien, "Media and Propaganda in Preparation for and During the Rwandan Genocide", study submitted to UNESCO by *Reporters sans frontières* and produced in collaboration with the Centre de Recherches Africaines. (Paris 1 – CNRS) (Paris: UNESCO, 30 April 1995).

AFTERWORD

Burundi

A confidential UN report, leaked to the press in mid-August 1996, has confirmed the role of the Burundian authorities and military in the failed *coup d'état* of 21 October 1993. It reports that "the assassination of President Ndadaye ... was planned in advance, as part of a *coup d'état* designed to overthrow him. The plan and execution of the coup were carried out by very senior General Staff officers".[1] It notes that at the time of Ndadaye's assassination, "no attempt was made to protect the President ... nobody [guarding him] was killed and no vehicles were damaged".[2] Moreover, the report unequivocally rejects the idea that the violence following the *putsch*, which claimed the lives of tens of thousands of Hutu and Tutsi, was the result of "supposed ancestral hatred between the Hutu and the Tutsi" or the "spontaneous rage" of peasants. Rather, it concludes that officials from the *Front démocratique du Burundi* (the Burundi Democratic Front — FRODEBU) were responsible for directing the violence against Tutsi immediately following the coup and that gendarmes and the mainly Tutsi army, which is close to the *Union pour le progrès national* (Union for National Progress — UPRONA), conducted indiscriminate reprisal killings of Hutu. The report found that "*ordinary Hutu peasants took part in the massacres only in response to the urging ... of their leaders who were present wherever the massacres occurred*" (italics added).[3]

From January 1994 Burundi was governed by a weak coalition government, in which the two successive Presidents came from FRODEBU, President Ndadaye's party, and Prime Ministers were appointed from UPRONA, the former ruling party. The majority of government posts were allocated to FRODEBU members and the rest were assigned to UPRONA and other opposition party representatives, a power-sharing agreement which was reversed on 25 July 1996 in the *coup d'état* led by Pierre Buyoya, who had previously served as President from 1987 to 1993.

Despite the role of the Burundian authorities and army in the killings of October 1993, and in the subsequent massacres which claimed the lives of approximately 156,000 people, the media has been increasingly blamed as a factor in the bloodshed. Burundian government officials, politicians and a local freedom of expression organization have mounted public pressure to ban extremist newspapers and jam broadcasts of Radio Democracy, a pirate radio station based in Zaire and controlled by Léonard Nyangoma's *Conseil national pour la défense de la démocratie* (National Council for the Defence of Democracy — CNDD). The *Forces pour la défense de la démocratie* (Forces for the Defence of Democracy — FDD), the armed wing of the CNDD, which was created in mid-1994, began to launch systematic guerrilla attacks into Burundi from Zaire in early 1995, and is believed to be responsible for widespread abuses of civilians.

The Burundian government has claimed that Radio Democracy, which began broadcasting on 13 July 1995, is "another RTLM" and has called for its banning. As a result of this campaign, and fearing "another Rwanda", international humanitarian and human rights groups, as well as UNESCO and other UN bodies, have focused their attention on the extremist media. In August 1995, the UN Sub-Commission on the Prevention of Discrimination and Protection of Minorities called for Radio Democracy to be dismantled.

On 1 November 1995 Burundi's National Communications Council declared Radio Democracy illegal and appealed to the international community for assistance in jamming the station. On 2 November 1995, Radio Burundi commented:

> At a time when the Burundian government is organizing awareness and peace campaigns all over the country to restore calm and security, this instrument of hatred and division may disrupt the process of rehabilitating a social fabric which is in tatters, as was the case with the regrettably well-known Mille Collines radio station [RTLM]. It is therefore a matter of urgency that Radio Democracy be dismantled so that peace is restored fully in Burundi and in the Great Lakes region. ...[4]

A few days later, UNESCO Director-General Federico Mayor sent an adviser to Zaire and Burundi in order to investigate the radio station. It was reported that UNESCO intended to "examine the possibilities of taking legal action to end the broadcasts of [the] pirate radio station".[5] In March 1996, the UN Security Council adopted a resolution inviting member states to dismantle the station. This was followed by a similar resolution by the UN Human Rights Commission in April.

Very little is known about the content of Radio Democracy broadcasts or the impact of the station and the "hate press" in Burundi. Recordings of the station made by the BBC Monitoring Service indicate a very different focus to that of RTLM, to which it has been constantly likened. Although Radio Democracy called on people to overthrow the former Burundian government, which it considered illegitimate, and to fight the Burundian army, there seems to be no clear evidence that the station has incited violence against civilians. In fact, a Radio Democracy broadcast on 13 July 1995 warned:

> Fight the enemies of Burundi, only attack military barracks and military positions. The crime of killing citizens, old people, the sick and infants should be left to the criminal [Jean] Bikomagu [Chief of Staff of the Burundian Armed Forces] and his army.[6]

Similarly, the move by the Burundian National Communication Council in March 1996 to ban, indefinitely, seven newspapers seems equally problematic. Although this measure was supported by *Reporters sans frontières* (RSF), UPRONA's hardline newspaper *L'Indépendant* was not among those banned, while FRODEBU's publication, *L'Aube de la Démocratie*, not considered extremist, was proscribed. Simon Kururu, Chairman of the National Communication Council explained the reasons for the bannings:

> Some newspapers were found to be causing disunity. Some were found to be spreading lies, others brought about hatred amongst the people. Some had not fulfilled all the requirements of the law.[7]

François Sendazirasa, President of the Burundian Association of Journalists (BAJ) commented, "I believe that the measure has only political objectives. It aims at protecting political officials who fear criticism, which cannot be supported by BAJ".[8] Journalists have continued to be harassed and arbitrarily detained in Burundi, yet their plight has not drawn as much international protest as the rise of "hate media" organs. Sendazirasa continued: "These people [journalists] are not dangerous, they are not criminals. Criminals are walking about freely. Journalists should not be handcuffed and imprisoned all the time".[9]

ARTICLE 19 hopes to publish a companion report on Violence and the Media in Burundi, *highlighting the context in which media control is exerted and its consequences. Like* Broadcasting Genocide, *this second report will document government propaganda on state radio, an institution which is in urgent need of reform, and the systematic harassment of journalists by the authorities. Within this context, ARTICLE 19 will present the rise of media organs which promote hate speech and violence, their links to political groups and, in some cases, to militias affiliated with political parties. Moreover, it will seek to gather first-hand information on the content of Radio Democracy's broadcasts and will examine the question of whether the international community should intervene to jam the pirate radio station. By separating the two reports we hope to emphasize that the tragedies of Rwanda and Burundi have quite different origins.*

Notes

[1] As cited in *Le Soir*, 14 Aug. 1996, in "Burundi: Belgian Newspaper Publishes part of the UN Report on October 1993 Events", *BBC Summary of World Broadcasts*, 16 Aug. 1996.

[2] Ibid.

[3] Ibid.

[4] Radio Burundi (French), 9430 GMT, 2 Nov. 1995, "UNESCO Head Promises to Help Burundi Dismantle 'Radio Station of Hatred'", in *BBC Summary of World Broadcasts*, 4 Nov. 1995.

[5] Pan-African news agency (PANA) cited by the KNA news agency, Nairobi (English), 1135 GMT, 4 Nov. 1995, in *BBC Summary of World Broadcasts*, 7 Nov. 1995.

[6] Radio Democracy (Kirundi), 13 July 1995, "Burundian radio calls on Burundians to fight Army, Support Hutu militias", *BBC Summary of World Broadcasts*, 9 Aug. 1995.

[7] As cited in Radio Burundi (Kirundi), 1030 GMT, 19 March 1996, "Burundi: Publication of Seven Private Newspapers Halted", *BBC Summary of World Broadcasts*, 21 March 1996.

[8] As cited in Radio Burundi (French), 1800 GMT, 19 March 1996, "Burundi: Journalists' Union Criticizes Suspension of Newspapers", *BBC Summary of World Broadcasts*, 21 March 1996.

[9] Ibid.

Appendix

RTLM Original Shareholders[1]

1. Isaac MULIHANO
2. Stanislas SIMBIZI
3. J Bosco BARAYAGWIZA
4. Félicien KABUGA
5. Charles NZABAGERAGEZA
6. Pasteur MUSABE
7. Ferdinand NAHIMANA
8. Rose USABUWERA
9. Marie BANZUBAZE
10. Drocella MUKAMBONERA
11. Bibiane NTEGAYIRE
12. Claude NDAMIYE
13. Joseph NZIRORERA
14. Télesphore BIZIMUNGU
15. Ignace TEMAHAGARI
16. Mathieu HAKIZAYEZU
17. J Damascène NDAGIJIMANA
18. Marc SINIYOBEWE
19. Ephrem NKEZABERA
20. Georges GAKERI
21. Joseph SERUGENDO
22. François SERUSHYANA
23. P Célestin HAGUMA
24. Victor KALISA
25. Alphonse NTIRIVAMUNDA
26. Augustin NGIRABATWARE
27. André NTAGERURA
28. Mme Laurence NYIRABAGENZI
29. Ernest BUROKO
30. J Baptiste NEMEYABAHIZI
31. Robert SIMBA
32. Cyprien NDAGIJIMANA
33. Simon BIKINDI

34. Bernard MANIRAGABA
35. Dieudonné NIYITEGEKA
36. Georges RUTAGANDA
37. Phénéas RUHUMULIZA
38. Bernardin NSENGAMUNGU
39. Daniel NTAWUMENYUMUNSI
40. Aaron NTIZIHABOSE
41. Déogratias NSABIMANA
42. Béatrice NYIRABALITONDA
43. Boniface RUCAGU
44. Jean HABYARIMANA
45. M Marthe MUJAWAYEZU
46. Froduald NTAWULIKURA
47. J Baptiste BAMWANGA
48. J M Vianney MVULIRWENANDE
49. Ammanuel NGIRWANABAGABO
50. J Bosco BICAMUMPAKA

Notes

[1] Reporters sans frontières, *Rwanda: médias de la haine ou presse démocratique, Rapport de mission 16-24 Sept. 1994* (Paris: RSF, 1994).

SELECTED ARTICLE 19 PUBLICATIONS

ARTICLE 19
INTERNATIONAL CENTRE AGAINST CENSORSHIP

Books

Fatal Silence? Freedom of Expression and the Right to Health in Burma
(Aug. 1996) 128pp., £5.99/$8.00

The Right to Know - Human Rights and Access to Reproductive Health Information (Aug.1995) 416pp., £18.00/$30.00

La Liberté de la Presse et de l'information au Maroc - limites et perspectives
(Joint report with OMDH,June 1995) 360pp. £5.99/$8.00, available from OMDH Morocco

Who Rules the Airwaves? Broadcasting in Africa (March 1995) 168pp., £9.99/$15.00

Fiction, Fact and the *Fatwa*: 2,000 Days of Censorship (Aug. 1994) 190pp., £7.95/$15.00

Guidelines for Election Broadcasting in Transitional Democracies (Aug. 1994) 124pp., £9.99/$15.00

Forging War: The Media in Serbia, Croatia and Bosnia-Hercegovina (May 1994) 288pp., £9.99/$15.00

Freedom of Expression Handbook: International and Comparative Law, Standards and Procedures (Aug. 1993) 322pp., £12.00/$20.00

Press Law and Practice: A Comparative Study of Press Freedom in European and Other Democracies (April 1993) 320pp., £12.00/$20.00

Striking a Balance: Hate Speech, Freedom of Expression and Non-discrimination (May 1992) 432pp., £9.95/$15.00

State of Fear: Censorship in Burma (Dec. 1991) 120pp., £3.95/$6.00

Starving in Silence: A Report on Famine and Censorship (April 1990) 146pp., £3.95/$6.00

Recent Reports

Muted Voices: Censorship and the Broadcast Media in Indonesia (June 1996) 24pp., £3.99/$6.00

China's Challenge: Freedom of Expression in Hong Kong - 1996 Annual Report (June 1996) 48pp., £3.99/$6.00

Silent War: Censorship and the Conflict in Sri Lanka (March 1996) £3.99/$6.00

The Johannesburg Principles: National Security, Freedom of Expression and Access to Information (Jan. 1996) 13pp.

A Travesty of Law and Justice: An Analysis of the Judgement in the Case of Ken Saro-Wiwa and others (Dec. 1995) 23pp., £3.00/$6.00

Northern Cameroon - Attacks on Freedom of Expression by Governmental and Traditional Authorities (July 1995) 36pp., £3.00/$5.00

Nigeria - Fundamental Human Rights Denied: Report of the Trial of Ken Saro-Wiwa and Others (June 1995) 36pp., £3.00/$6.00

Censorship in Kenya: Government Critics Face the Death Sentence (March 1995) 40pp., £3.99/$6.00

Censorship Prevails: Political Deadlock and Economic Transition in Burma (March 1995) 60pp., £3.99/$6.00

Censorship News Reports

MOZAMBIQUE: Freedom of Expression and "The Vote for Peace" (Oct. 1995)

COTE D'IVOIRE: Silencing the Media - Censorship and the Elections (Sept. 1995)

INDONESIA: Surveillance and Suppression - The Legacy of the 1965 Coup (Sept. 1995)

INDONESIA: The Press on Trial (Aug. 1995)

SRI LANKA: Words into Action - Censorship and Media Reform (March 1995)

ALGERIA: Secret Decree - New Attack on the Media (Nov. 1994)

GAMBIA: Democracy Overturned - Violations of Freedom of Expression (Dec. 1994)

MOZAMBIQUE: Freedom of Expression and the Elections (Oct. 1994)

MALAWI: Freedom of Expression - The Elections and the Need for Media Reform (July 1994)

MALAWI's Elections: Media Monitoring, Freedom of Expression and Intimidation
(April 1994)

JORDAN: Democratization without Press Freedom (March 1994)

ALGERIA: Assassination in the Name of Religion (Dec. 1993)

TUNISIA: The Press in Tunisia - Plus ça change (Nov. 1993)

KENYA: Shooting the Messenger (Oct. 1993)

Bulletin

The ARTICLE 19 Newsletter, published 3 times per year. The Bulletin is available for an annual subscription of £15/US$25 which includes membership.

Subscriptions

An Annual Subscription to all ARTICLE 19 publications is available at a cost including postage of £75 (UK) or £85/US$130 (Overseas).

Please add the following to your payment for postage and packing:

UK and EC countries - Orders under £25/US$40 add 20% of total; orders over £25, add 10%.

Overseas - add 50% of total for airmail; 20% for surface mail.

*** Only cheques drawn in UK £ sterling or US dollars can be accepted.***

All publications are available from:

ARTICLE 19
The International Centre Against Censorship

33 Islington High Street, London N1 9LH, United Kingdom
Tel: (0171) 278 9292 Fax: (0171) 713 1356
E-mail: article19@gn.apc.org

Trade Distribution:
Central Books
99 Wallis Road, London, E9 5LN
Tel: 0181-986 4854 Fax: 0181-533 5821

ARTICLE 19

The International Centre Against Censorship

ARTICLE 19 takes its name and purpose from Article 19 of the Universal Declaration of Human Rights.

> *Everyone has the right to freedom of opinion and expression; this right includes freedom to hold opinions without interference and to seek, receive and impart information and ideas through any media and regardless of frontiers.*

ARTICLE 19 works impartially and systematically to oppose censorship worldwide. We work on behalf of victims of censorship — individuals who are physically attacked, killed, unjustly imprisoned, restricted in their movements or dismissed from their jobs; print and broadcast media which are censored, banned or threatened; organizations, including political groups or trades unions, which are harassed, suppressed or silenced.

ARTICLE 19's programme of research, publication, campaign and legal intervention addresses censorship in its many forms. We monitor individual countries' compliance with international standards protecting the right to freedom of expression and work at the governmental and inter-governmental level to promote greater respect for this fundamental right.

ARTICLE 19 has established a growing international network of concerned individuals and organizations who promote awareness of censorship issues and take action on individual cases.

ARTICLE 19 is a non-governmental organization, entirely dependent on donations (UK Charity No. 327421). For more information contact:

ARTICLE 19
Lancaster House, 33 Islington High Street, London N1 9LH
Tel: 0171 278 9292 Fax: 0171 713 1356, E-mail: article19@gn.apc.org